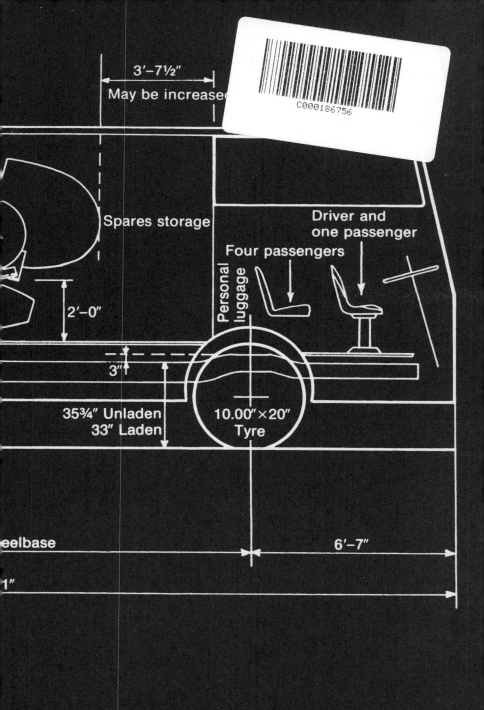

3'–7½"
May be increased

C000186756

Spares storage

Driver and
one passenger

Four passengers

Personal
luggage

2'–0"

3"

35¾" Unladen
33" Laden

10.00"×20"
Tyre

eelbase

6'–7"

1"

The Last Road Race

Also by Richard Williams

The Death of Ayrton Senna
Racers
Enzo Ferrari: A Life
The View From the High Board

THE LAST ROAD RACE

THE 1957 PESCARA GRAND PRIX

Richard Williams

Photographs by Bernard Cahier

To Trevor —

Richard Williams.

Weidenfeld & Nicolson

LONDON

First published in Great Britain in 2004
by Weidenfeld & Nicolson

A CIP catalogue record for this book
is available from the British Library.

ISBN 0 297 64558 7

Typeset by Selwood Systems, Midsomer Norton

Printed in Great Britain by
Butler & Tanner Ltd, Frome and London

Weidenfeld & Nicolson

The Orion Publishing Group Ltd
Orion House
5 Upper Saint Martin's Lane
London, WC2H 9EA

Contents

'I thought it was fantastic. It was just like being a kid, out for a burn-up. A wonderful feeling. What racing's all about.'

Stirling Moss

'Those road courses were bloody dangerous and nasty, all of them. And Pescara was the worst.'

Jack Brabham

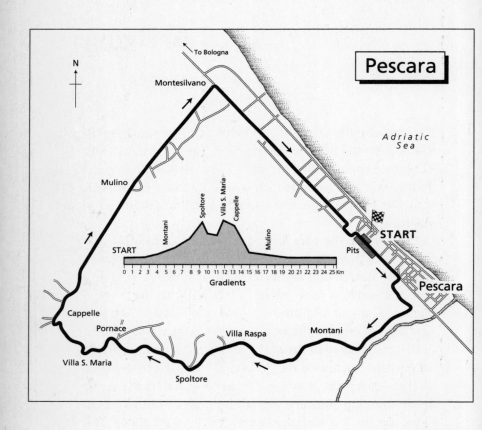

N

To Bologna

Montesilvano

Mulino

Adriatic Sea

Spoltore

Villa S. Maria

Cappelle

Montani

Villa S. Maria

Mulino

START

Gradients

0 1 2 3 4 5 6 7 8 9 10 11 12 13 14 15 16 17 18 19 20 21 22 23 24 25 Km

START

Pits

Pescara

Cappelle

Pornace

Villa S. Maria

Spoltore

Villa Raspa

Montani

Pescara

1

Arriving

On the morning of the race, Stirling Moss woke at seven o'clock. By the time he had dressed, eaten breakfast with his father and travelled the short distance from their hotel to the track, the sun was high in the sky above the Adriatic and the temperature was already heading towards 100 degrees.

One by one the cars arrived at the pits, driven by their mechanics from the local garages in which the teams had set up a base of operations so far from home: a swarm of ten Maseratis, a lone scarlet Ferrari, three sleek green Vanwalls, a pair of little hunchbacked Coopers. Many of the drivers and mechanics had been kept awake by the late-night display of fireworks with which the inhabitants of Pescara celebrated the holiday of Ferragosto, the feast of the assumption. Now the competitors clustered together in the burning sunshine between the pits and the grandstand on the Via Adriatica, ready for the start at half past nine.

Thinking of the heat when he got himself ready that morning, Moss had chosen a pale blue short-sleeved shirt made out of thin cotton, with a sort of waffle pattern that allowed the air to circulate. It had kept him cool a few months earlier in the blistering heat of the Florida desert during the Sebring sports car race. With the shirt he had a pair of light cotton trousers, bearing the logo of the Avon tyre company, cinched in with a broad belt. He wore his driving gloves, with thin leather palms and knitted string backs. He had his familiar pure white helmet – from Herbert Johnson, the Mayfair hatters – and his oval, leather-trimmed goggles. Bright flags hung limp in the still air as he greeted his team-mates.

Traffic had been pouring into Pescara all night, drawn like moths to the fireworks. Across the mountains from Rome they came, passing through the hilltop town of L'Aquila and traversing the vast moonlit plateau south of the Gran Sasso d'Italia. Others came from the northern cities of Milan and Turin, heading for the sea along the Via Emilia before turning south at Ravenna down the ancient, arrow-straight coast road. Thousands more made their way by train, alighting at Pescara's main station, a stone's throw from the track.

The town itself seemed barely changed since the 19th century. It had escaped bombing and shelling, but barely a dozen years after the end of the Second World War some abandoned buildings still showed the signs of hand-to-hand combat. Most of the streets were cobbled. Despite its status as a popular seaside town, the hotels were generally small, family-run affairs.

Some of the arriving spectators took their seats in the large temporary grandstand erected opposite the pits, or in smaller tribunes near the artificial chicane a few hundred yards before the start and finish line. Many more parked their cars in the villages around the circuit, finding a vantage point on a piece of hillside overlooking a bend in the road and preparing for a day of picnicking and noise and excitement.

By nine o'clock, half an hour before the start, the course was closed. The last straw bales had been pushed into position, piled across junctions to mark the direction of the circuit. In the villages, kerbstones had been given a final lick of black and white paint. Dogs, sheep, cows, donkeys and oxen were shut away. Those whose houses abutted the track settled themselves by the windows or in the shade of the doorways, ready for a wonderful free show. Around 200,000 people were said to be in attendance; this was more than twice the town's population, already swollen by thousands who had been spending the holiday weekend by the seaside in Pescara or one of its neighbouring resorts.

There was plenty of space for all of them. The circuit, over twenty-five kilometres in length, could have absorbed many more spectators as it passed through one major town, three villages and half a dozen hamlets. This was a round of the official Formula One world championship, but there could be no attempt to restrict admission to paying customers. Pescara represented a world far away from the turnstiles and paddock passes of Monza or Silverstone. For one weekend only, grand prix racing was returning to the earliest days of its existence, half a century before.

'I love road racing,' Stirling Moss said, slipping in and out of the present tense as he sat in his London home more than four decades later. 'Circuits like that, when the weather's good and so on, you suddenly find yourself on the most fantastic piece of road, very demanding, and to me that was what road racing was all about. You'd go to

Spa, which was a proper road, and the Nürburgring ... those, really and truly, were what motor racing was. You'd go to a town like Aix les Bains and you'd get there on the Thursday and they'd set up the circuit with straw bales to show you where it went. Usually it was just around one part of the town, and practice would start and the clerk of the course would go round to see that it was all right. You'd practise for a couple of hours and then they'd take the straw bales away and life would go back to normal. That's what it was.'

And this, one August morning in 1957, may have been the highest pinnacle of road racing: a farewell to grand prix racing in the grand manner, although no one saw it that way at the time. But Denis Jenkinson, the Continental correspondent of *Motor Sport*, would make a profound point when, writing on the night after the prizes had been presented, he described the 25th Gran Premio di Pescara to his readers as a battle 'not between driver and driver, or even between car and car [but] between the combination of car and driver against natural surroundings'.

There had never been a race for world championship points at Pescara before, and there would never be another. Never again would a *grande épreuve*, as the championship races were known, take place in an environment so consistent with the manner of the sport's formative years, so evocative of the exhilarating combination of adventure and danger that had given motor racing its allure before technology and a growing awareness of personal safety took it into another realm.

Nowadays racing drivers park their executive jets at the airport nearest to the circuit and then hop into a helicopter for the last bit of the journey. In 1957 Moss arrived at Pescara in a rented Fiat 1100 which he had driven across Italy from the airport at Rome, with his father in the passenger seat. His team-mate Tony Brooks came all the way from England in a factory-fresh Hillman Minx coupé, sharing the wheel with Roy Salvadori, one of the Cooper team's drivers, who was testing the car on behalf of a monthly magazine, *Autocourse*. In Milan they stopped to pick up Brooks's Italian fiancée. Stuart Lewis-Evans, who had recently joined Moss and Brooks in the Vanwall team, covered the same journey in a Nash Metropolitan coupé, a funny little Anglo-American two-seater aimed, perhaps prematurely, at a post-war public just rediscovering frivolity and style. Handling and speed were not its strong points, but, according to the American photographer Jesse Alexander, Lewis-Evans was extremely proud of it.

'It was red and white,' his friend and adviser Bernie Ecclestone remembered. 'We used to use it all the time. We raced Graham Hill at Spa in it once, at night with no lights. Graham was in his Austin A35. Those were the mad days. I remember getting shot at in that Nash at Spa, when the Belgian police thought we should stop for some reason or another and Stuart didn't, so they let off a few shots in our direction.'

Jack Brabham, due to drive alongside Salvadori in the Cooper team, reached distant Pescara by means that would make today's drivers even more astonished. 'I drove the transporter down there,' he said. 'It was a long way and they needed more than one driver.' Brabham had been making himself useful as an auxiliary mechanic at the little Cooper factory in Surbiton since his arrival from Australia in 1955, and there was never any doubt of his willingness to perform whatever task was necessary to get the cars on to the grid.

By comparison with the drivers, some of the better-known journalists arrived in style. Denis Jenkinson drove down in his Porsche 356, still a relatively exotic sight on public roads. Jesse Alexander, who was freelancing for *Sports Cars Illustrated*, arrived from his home near Interlaken in another Porsche. Bernard Cahier, a young French photojournalist who had started to contribute grand prix reports to the US magazine *Road & Track*, came across the Alps from his home in Evian in his Renault Dauphine, which had already seen service in the previous year's Mille Miglia. 'The drive to Pescara was nice because I took some of the same roads on which I'd competed,' he said. Michael Tee, a young photographer whose father owned *Motor Sport*, flew from London to Rome and then picked up a ride across the mountains on the flight carrying the day's post to Pescara, in a single-engined plane with enough space for several sacks of mail and one passenger.

Moss had raced at Pescara once before, and loved it. Among those seeing it for the first time that year, reactions were mixed. Today, the four drivers who survive from that morning in 1957 are split into two camps. Roy Salvadori would remain dismissive. 'I thought it was a horrible circuit,' he said 45 years later. Jack Brabham shared his teammate's view. 'Those road courses were bloody dangerous and nasty, nearly all of them, and Pescara was the worst,' he said. 'I can't remember anything good about it at all. Oh, yes I can. I went for a swim in the sea and it was like being in a warm bath. And the hotel was OK.' Tony Brooks, however, was in Moss's camp, just as he had been in the race. 'Fantastic,' he said. 'A real race circuit. To me, grand prix racing is road racing, and anything less than that is nothing like as rewarding or satisfying. It was a great driver's challenge. And it goes back to how grand prix racing started, city to city. It was new to Stuart and me, but I knew there had been lots of races there before.'

In fact Pescara had an illustrious racing history which could be traced back to 1924 and the first running of the Coppa Acerbo, named after a Great War hero. That race was won by a young driver called Enzo Ferrari. In the years immediately before the Second World War there had been marvellous contests featuring the great cars and drivers of the day. Summer after summer, the sight of Rudi Caracciola and Manfred von Brauchitsch in the Mercedes and Tazio Nuvolari and Bernd Rosemeyer in the Auto Unions had brought the thunderous sensations of a golden age of motor racing to this Adriatic town. After the war there were still races, and sometimes they even attracted leading drivers; but whereas the Coppa Acerbo had been a fixture in the diaries of the major teams, the inauguration of an official world championship, with a points system and a fixed calendar, pushed the annual race in Pescara out of the headlines. The town's name survived in the minds of motor racing enthusiasts mainly as one of the most significant locations on the route of the Mille Miglia, the great round-Italy sports car race, which had been established in 1927. In the later editions of the Mille Miglia, the town of Pescara was where the cars finally slowed after the long flat-out dash down the coast before turning sharp right and heading for Rome, the halfway point of the race.

But 1957 was different. The Suez crisis of the previous

year had brought petrol rationing and economic uncertainty. Two rounds of the championship, in Belgium and Holland, were cancelled at the last minute amid rancorous disputes. Both sets of organisers had asked the teams to accept reduced appearance fees, and each was rebuffed. Faced by the prospect of a championship reduced to a mere half-dozen rounds, and with huge gaps between races, the sporting department of the Fédération Internationale de l'Automobile looked around for possible replacements. They found one in Pescara, where the local automobile club was anxious to revive its old traditions and enthusiastic about the idea of regaining its former stature.

The people, getting on for a quarter of a million of them, who saw the race at Pescara in 1957, whether inhabitants of the town or visitors from a far corner of northern Europe, were privileged to witness an event on which the history of motor racing pivoted. This was the last time thoroughbred grand prix cars would race together over a true road circuit, meaning a circuit formed from roads in daily use, with no artificial features, not even permanent pits or grandstands. At 15.99 miles from start to finish, Pescara was and would remain the longest circuit in the history of the world championship. But there was much more to it than that.

To those who really understand motor racing, its fascination exists not just in the appeal of man or machine but in the constantly shifting balance between the two. How much is any success due to the driver, and how much to the car? On one particular day we can say that a talented man has overcome the limitations of his machinery; on another that a perfect machine has compensated for the flawed contribution of the man. Sometimes the driver and the car appear to be matched, but the equation is never quite balanced, or not for long. Within the myriad imbalances and uncertainties lies the allure of a complex sport whose many requirements for success include the apparently conflicting demands of scientific rigour and raw courage.

On a purely human level, the 1957 Pescara Grand Prix offered a competition between the most successful driver of all time, Juan Manuel Fangio, and the man expected to be his successor, Stirling Moss. It was the season during which, at the age of 46, Fangio produced the greatest performance of his career, and in which he was to set a mark of five world championships that would not be equalled for more than 40 years. For Moss, aged 27, it was the year in which he would demonstrate beyond doubt his right to assume the mantle of the great Argentine, his friend and mentor.

But there were other conflicts going on. In terms of cars, the race was set up as a battle between the red cars of Italy and the green cars of Britain, between the old order of continental Europe and an emerging power with very different methods and priorities. But there were two additional sets of struggles. One was between the two teams of red cars: the first, Ferrari, which sent only a single car to Pescara, would still be a dominant force in grand prix racing almost half a century later; the second, Maserati, which in one way or another provided 10 of the 16 cars that formed the grid in Pescara, would be out of grand prix racing as a real force by the end of the year. The other internal battle was between the two teams of green cars, Vanwall and Cooper, representing in the clearest possible perspective the past and the future of the sport's technology.

And, as it turned out, the past and the future were both winners that year at Pescara.

History

'Pescara was a fascinating place,' Bernard Cahier recalled. 'An old town by the sea, great atmosphere, lots of orchards.' Yet it is not a place that often crosses the mind of the average Italian, particularly if he or she comes from the prosperous north. Nor is it on the itinerary of international travellers (it rates no mention at all, for example, in the green Michelin guide to Italy). Located along the straight line of the Adriatic coast, roughly halfway between Rimini and Bari, it is simply the largest and liveliest of the many rather featureless seaside spots favoured by the inhabitants of the region (just to the north are a group of resorts known as the *sette sorelle*, or seven sisters, which form an easterly counterpart to the far more fashionable strip of resorts running down the Ligurian sea to Viareggio).

Known to the Romans as Piscaria, Pescara is the principal coastal town of Abruzzo, the province named after the mountain range which sits astride the saddle of Italy, where the peaks reach around 2500 metres. Fishing, agriculture and sheep farming were the subsistence economies of the region for most of the twentieth century, and the vast gulf between the landowners and the peasants made the Abruzzi fertile ground for the rise of Fascism in the 1920s. But Pescara had its own brigade of partisans who fought to free the country from the grip of the *nazifascisti*, and by the end of the war much of the town had been damaged in the street fighting between Hitler's retreating armies and the Allied forces. In the early 1950s tourists began to return to its beach, which is sixteen kilometres long. To cater to their needs, bars and restaurants and, eventually, discotheques began to spring up along the front.

Its two most famous sons both made their living with words. One, Ennio Flaiano, was a screenwriter. In the 1950s and 1960s, when Italy was making a vital contribution to world cinema, Flaiano collaborated with Federico Fellini on the maestro's most significant films, including *Il Vitelloni*, *La Strada*, *La Dolce Vita* and *Otto e mezzo*. The other, Gabriele D'Annunzio, was one of the most famous Italians of the last hundred years. Poet, playwright, politician, soldier, aviator, nationalist, Fascist sympathiser, Prince of Monte Nevoso and president of the Italian Royal Academy, D'Annunzio attended the University of Rome and ended his days in 1938 at his villa in the gentler climate of Lake Garda, at the age of 75. Nevertheless the hermitages and the frescoes of Pescara and its surrounding towns had provided him with the inspiration for such classics as *Il Trionfo della Morte*, *Il Piacere* and *La Figlia di Jorio*, not to mention the collection of short stories titled *Novelle della Pescara*.

When Pescara held its first race, in 1924, the trophy was named after another native son. Tito Acerbo, born in nearby Loreto Aprutino in 1890, was a captain in the Brigati Sassari of the 152nd infantry regiment when he met his death at

Croce di Piave in the Dolomites on 16 June 1918, in one of the bloodiest engagements of the war against the Austro-Hungarian army. His older brother, Giacomo, a university professor turned Fascist politician who rose to become Mussolini's last finance minister in 1943, dedicated the Coppa Acerbo to his brother; not until after the war, when Mussolini's politics were out of fashion, did the name of the race become the Circuito di Pescara, or the Gran Premio di Pescara.

The first race took place on 13 July 1924, two months after Mussolini's coalition had won 65 per cent of the popular vote in an election which took place under rules drawn up by Giacomo Acerbo, and one month after Enzo Ferrari had met Tazio Nuvolari for the first time in front of the basilica of Sant'Apollinare in Classe in Ravenna, where the pits for the Circuito del Savio had been set up. They were professional racing drivers, and history records that Ferrari, driving a powerful Alfa Romeo RL, finished first, ahead of Nuvolari, at the wheel of a little Chiribiri in one of his first races on four wheels. A week later they finished in the same order in the Circuito del Polesine, and became friends. Ten days later the prominent socialist politician Giacomo Matteoti was kidnapped and murdered by Mussolini's thugs; outside the fast-evolving little world of Italian motor sport, the country was in turmoil.

Ferrari made it a hat-trick in Pescara, the best run of his career as a driver, although it was not against the most impressive opposition: second and third were Bonmartini in a Mercedes and Beria d'Argentina in an SPA. What was impressive was the circuit, which measured 25.578 kilometres, or 15.99 miles. To some observers it appeared to constitute a miniature version of the great Targa Florio, which had been held since 1907 over the narrow unmade roads of Sicily's Madonie mountains – although, unlike Count Vincenzo Florio's epic race, it was run in a clockwise direction.

Pescara's starting line was close to the town centre, on the Via Adriatica, the Roman road that runs parallel to the seafront. The pits were located on the landward side, with the mountains behind them, while the temporary covered grandstands had their backs to the sea. Half a mile from the start the circuit turned sharp right just before the railway station, then left and right again before heading through the outskirts of the town, with the Pescara river on the left and a hospital on the right. It started to climb as it passed through the suburbs of Montani and Villa Raspa, emerging into open country as the road narrowed and the village of Spoltore came into view. After passing between the stone church and houses, the circuit descended and then climbed again to reach its highest point on the winding road through the hamlets of Pornase and Villa St Maria before plunging down to Cappelle sul Tavo, where a spectacular 180-degree hairpin bend, with the natural grandstand of a high earth bank on the outside, brought the cars back to face the sea. From Capelle they dropped back down to the coast on a five-mile straight following the course of another small river, the Saline, interrupted only by a kink at Mulino – the mill – and running past the village of Montesilvano on the right. On this fast downhill stretch in later years the timekeepers set up a 'flying kilometre', over which they could measure the maximum speed of the cars: a prize of 200,000 lire, or about £115, was given to the driver of the fastest car. At the bottom of the hill the cars braked for a 90-degree right-hander near the railway station at Montesilvano Marina, bringing them back on to the coast road, with another five-mile straight along the Via Adriatica before they reached the pits once again.

'Here I made my name as a driver,' Ferrari was to recollect. He had not been expecting to win; his friend and team-mate Giuseppe Campari, a part-time opera singer, had been entered with a new Alfa Romeo P2, a pure-blooded racing machine, and Ferrari ordered his riding mechanic, Eugenio Siena, to keep a look-out for the faster machine so that he could let it go by. But Campari had retired with gearbox trouble, and hid his car up a side-street in order not to alert their rivals. Somewhat to his surprise, Ferrari was able to win at an average speed of 104.5kph, or just under 65mph, over ten laps of a course made hazardous by clouds of dust and a spray of pebbles from the unmade roads. And, as a reporter from the magazine *Autosprint* observed, the cars wore grooves in the curves which grew deeper as the race wore on. Ferrari's lap times were between 14min 30sec and 14min 56sec, a pioneering effort which won him the gold Coppa Acerbo, 5000 lire, the king's medal and the title of *Cavaliere*.

But Ferrari's new-found reputation as an ace driver was barely to outlast the month. On 3 August he was due to compete for the first time as a member of Alfa Romeo's full grand prix team for the Grand Prix d'Europe, to be held at Lyon. After Pescara he took the train from Milan to France along with Campari and Antonio Ascari. With his friend Luigi Bazzi in the mechanic's seat, he tested the car over the circuit on 18 and 22 July. But then, suddenly and mysteriously, he returned to Italy and would not race again for two years. Some said he was frightened by the car's power; others that his new wife had dissuaded him from driving.

His own version was that he was suffering from an unspecified illness that would afflict him again later in his life.

The inaugural race was such a success that Giacomo Acerbo and the burghers of Pescara made plans for an annual event, to be held in the week of Ferragosto. The length of the race was doubled, from 159 to 317 miles; the winner was Ginaldi in a Bugatti, and the same marque triumphed again in 1926, with Spinozzi as the driver. Campari won the races of 1927, 1928 and 1930, on an Alfa Romeo each time, with another great Italian driver, Achille Varzi, taking the 1929 race in a Maserati. When Nuvolari and Luigi Fagioli completed Alfa Romeo's run of success in 1931 and 1932, over a distance reduced to 190 miles, their cars were entered by the newly formed Scuderia Ferrari.

Acerbo also expanded the event, turning Ferragosto into a festival of motor sport – a *Manifestazione Automobilistica*, as the posters said. From 1926 there was a race for voiturettes, as smaller racing cars with 1100cc engines were known. Stefanelli's Bugatti was the first winner, followed over the next few years by various Salmsons and Amilcars, the MG Magnettes of Whitney Straight and Hugh Hamilton, and the ERA and Delage of Richard Seaman, the young English star whose victories in 1935 and 1936 helped consolidate his growing reputation on the Continent. When Straight, a young American sportsman, arrived at Pescara in his Puss Moth biplane and drove his little MG to victory, the Italians would not believe that his car could derive so much speed from an engine of only 1.1 litres. So they stripped it down after the race, only to admit that the English car satisfied the regulations. To add to Pescara's entertainment, in 1934 there was a 24-hours race for sports cars, the Targa Abruzzo, emulating the hugely popular event at Le Mans, which had been held for the first time in 1923 and had attracted support from manufacturers hoping to display the speed and durability of their road cars. Franco Cortese and Francesco Severi took the inaugural victory in an Alfa. They won it again in 1935, after which the duration was reduced to six hours, Cortese winning twice more. The final pre-war Targa Abruzzo, in 1938, was scheduled for eight hours' duration and was won by Righetti and Rangoni, yet again in an Alfa.

Enzo Ferrari had noted Acerbo's enthusiasm for motor sport, and the meticulous care with which he organised the event. 'He had, for instance, an absolute mania for the maximum permitted number of cars on the start line – twenty-four for the grand prix and sixty for the twelve-hours [sic] race,' Ferrari wrote in his memoirs. 'On one occasion he rang me up only a week before the race to tell me he needed eleven cars to make up the quota. I was dumbfounded: wherever was I going to get eleven Alfa Romeos from? And yet I had to find them somehow. Acerbo was like that.'

The main attraction, the Coppa Acerbo itself, was going from strength to strength. A giant portrait of Mussolini now hung alongside the hand-operated leader board which confronted the spectators in the expanded main grand-stand, a profusion of flags decorated the pits, and adver-tising signs for commercial sponsors – the manufacturers of tyres, petroleum products and spark plugs – had begun to make their appearance. A huge banner hung across the track, bearing the word TRAGUARDO, or 'finishing line', with discreet Fiat logos on either side. In front of the grandstand, a row of sandbags, about two feet high, marked the edge of the track. The annual crowd was estimated at around a quarter of a million.

In 1934, when a new formula was introduced which restricted the cars to a maximum weight of 750kg but with no limits on engine size, the state-sponsored German teams arrived with the cars that were to become known as 'silver arrows'. Fagioli, born not far away, up the coast near Ancona, drove a Mercedes-Benz to victory in 1934. The speed of the German cars was enough to persuade the organisers to introduce chicanes into the long straights, in an attempt to slow them down. But the following year it was the turn of an Auto Union, with Varzi at the wheel, after a race of high drama and tragedy. Rudolf Caracciola, the Mercedes team leader, left the track at high speed, hurtled across a couple of fields and overturned, without injury to the driver. When Louis Chiron came into the pits in one of Scuderia Ferrari's Alfas, his car caught fire and the driver's blazing overalls had to be extinguished. His team-mate Guy Moll was less lucky. Running in second place and lapping the Auto Union of Ernst Henne while both cars were passing through the flying kilometre at over 160mph, the Scuderia's 25-year-old Algerian star felt a gust of wind catch his Alfa Tipo B. The car veered to the right, ran along the verge and into a ditch for 50 yards, hit a stone wall and left the road, somersaulting and cutting through telephone wires before smashing into the side of a house. The driver was thrown against a concrete post and killed instantly, ending a career bright with promise. In second place, behind Varzi, came Bernd Rosemeyer, a motorbike ace driving an Auto Union in only his first season of racing on four wheels. Rosemeyer had left the road at high speed during the race, flying over a ditch and passing between a telegraph pole and a bridge parapet before regaining the track. After the race the gap between the parapet and the pole was measured by Dr Ferdinand Porsche, the Auto Union's designer; it was found to be five centimetres wider than the car.

The brilliant Rosemeyer won in 1936, when Seaman won the voiturette race for the second year in a row and was given a works three-litre, straight-eight Maserati for the main event. 'I did not get very far,' the Englishman wrote to his friend, the photographer George Monkhouse, 'for in the course of three laps the filler-cap sprung open, the mirror fell off, a front brake locked and the water temperature went to 110 deg C, and the engine on to seven jugs. It is the last time I drive a works Maserati!' Prince Chula of Siam, accompanying his brother, the driver B. Bira, wrote of their decision to stay in the biggest hotel in town: 'We found it exceedingly difficult to sleep. The hotel was near a goods yard and shunting appeared to be going on all night; whenever we had a few moments' respite, then a donkey would begin braying. Seaman had been there before, and knew better. He stayed at a tiny hotel by the sea.'

Rosemeyer won again in 1937, by which time the Auto Unions and Mercedes were reaching 200mph on the long straight between Montesilvano and the pits, despite the inclusion of the chicanes, which were not fiddly little things but rather more like detours, in the manner of the swimming pool complex introduced at Monaco in the 1970s. Rosemeyer had arrived in Pescara at the controls of a rakish Messerschmitt Taifun belonging to his new wife, the aviator Elly Beinhorn. During the race he slid wide and hit a paving stone, but was unaware that he had dislodged a wheel nut until his right rear wheel came rolling past him as he pulled into an emergency tyre and refuelling depot set up by the team on the back section of the circuit. The mechanics replaced it and he sprinted away to resume his victorious drive. 'I was worried that von Brauchitsch was catching up,' he said afterwards, 'so I had to hurry.' Seaman, who had joined the Mercedes team that season and was only just recovering from various minor injuries suffered in a crash at the Nürburgring, experienced a fright during practice when a front brake locked as he was negotiating a bend near Cappelle at high speed. His car hit one of the many solid kerbside marker stones, smashing the front suspension, pushing the nearside front wheel back into the bodywork and dislodging the engine mountings: a write-off.

George Monkhouse visited the race for the first time that year with his friend Seaman, and was on the spot to record the wreck of the Mercedes near Cappelle. His description of the visit during the Ferragosto week is a classic of English distaste. 'One is lucky to get anything to eat at all or even a bed,' he wrote. 'I was singularly unlucky in my choice of the latter. I learnt afterwards from Earl Howe that I had myself entirely to blame. He goes to Pescara equipped with a mosquito net, two Flit sprays, and a large pot of Flit ointment, which makes the human body a less delectable morsel to such insect life.'

Rosemeyer never had the chance to complete his hat-trick. By the time the German teams arrived for the last time in 1938 he was dead, killed on a closed autobahn during a record attempt in a streamlined Auto Union. Caracciola won the race, and it was the turn of his Mercedes team-mate Hermann Lang to leap from his car with overalls ablaze after shrapnel from a blown engine had severed a petrol pipe. Lightly singed, Lang was given a lift back to the pits by René Dreyfus, whose two-seater Delehaye was suffering from gearbox problems.

The Germans never returned. In 1939, with war in Europe only a month away, the Coppa Acerbo was held for cars of 1.5 litres maximum capacity, in common with all other Italian grands prix that year, the idea being to give local boys a chance. Clemente Biondetti led an Alfa Romeo clean sweep, but the event was marred by two more fatalities: those of Giordano Aldrighetti, who crashed his Alfa in practice, and of Catullo Lami, who had qualified for the race only by finishing in the top three of the voiturette race in his little Maserati earlier in the day.

When the race returned after the war, it was with a different title. 'I have noticed that the name Acerbo is no longer connected with the event,' Ferrari wrote. 'One might say it has been purged from it. This, I feel, is taking things a bit too far, for the race was actually named after the minister's brother, who was not a Fascist but a heroic soldier who was decorated for valour in the First World War.'

The first post-war race was for sports cars, and was won by Vincenzo Auricchio's pretty little 1100cc Stanguellini, a typical Fiat-based special of the time, built by an ingenious constructor whose factory was in the city of Modena, already famous for its involvement with the Scuderia Ferrari and, since the war, the Maserati concern. Cars bearing Ferrari's own name made their appearance at Pescara in 1948, one of them finishing second, to Alberto Ascari's Maserati, in the hands of Count Bruno Sterzi. Giovanni Bracco (Maserati) and Franco Rol (Alfa Romeo) were other winners of these races in the immediate post-war years before, in 1950, the big single-seaters returned to Pescara.

That year, the inaugural season of the FIA world championship, the works Alfa Romeos were invincible in the hands of Fagioli, Juan Manuel Fangio and Giuseppe Farina, the last of whom went on to win the title. Pescara was not included in the championship calendar; nevertheless the Alfa team made the trip, as they had to other non-championship races at Pau, San Remo, Angoulême and Geneva. Fagioli and Fangio were running away with the race, as usual, against negligible opposition from the Maserati and Talbot teams when, on the last lap, one of the front springs of Fagioli's car broke. With his left front wheel leaning inwards and rubbing against the bodywork, Fagioli stopped. So did Fangio, who had been following some distance behind. He asked his team-mate what had happened. 'I'm out,' Fagioli said. Fangio told him to keep going, and that he would follow him: an extraordinarily chivalrous gesture. As Fagioli's crippled car limped down the long descent to Montesilvano, one wheel wobbling perilously, Fangio kept an eye on his mirrors, looking for Rosier's third-placed Talbot. When they were almost at the final chicane, the pale blue car came into sight. It was gaining fast, and Fagioli gestured Fangio to go ahead, lest neither of them should win. Fangio took the flag for his eighth win of the season in the Alfa 158, and also collected the money for the flying kilometre, having been timed at 192mph. Less than 200 metres from the line, Rosier shot past Fagioli to claim second place.

Midway through 1951, Ferrari at last got the better of Alfa Romeo in a world championship grand prix. At Silverstone on 14 July, José Froilàn Gonzàlez muscled his big

4.5-litre Ferrari 375 past the four supercharged Alfas to take an historic victory. At the Nürburgring two weeks later Alberto Ascari rubbed salt into the wound, and a fortnight after that Gonzàlez celebrated Ferrari's new ascendancy with a win at Pescara, on this occasion in the absence of the Alfas and after the retirement of his team-mates, Ascari and Villoresi.

By this time the spectators in the grandstand could no longer look over the low temporary pits and see wooded hillsides. As Pescara began to grow during the first stages of Italy's post-war reconstruction, and as the natives of the Abruzzi began to move down from the mountains into the towns, houses and shops were starting to line both sides of the Via Adriatica.

In 1952 and 1953 the Gran Premio di Pescara was held for sports cars, with victory going to Ferraris on both occasions: to Umberto Maglioli and Mike Hawthorn in 1952 and Giovanni Bracco and Paolo Marzotto the following year. A year later, however, the Formula One cars returned, now governed by new regulations restricting cars to engines of 2.5 litres unsupercharged or 750cc supercharged. Once more the sound of grand prix engines echoed through the villages of the Abruzzi foothills. And at around nine o'clock on the evening of Thursday, 12 August 1954, Stirling Moss arrived in Pescara for the first time.

3

Moss

Stirling Moss opened the door of the little mews house in Shepherds Market, just off Park Lane, where he has lived since 1958. Then he settled himself behind the desk in his small office, with its glass case full of models of the cars he once drove and, mounted high on the wall, two mementos of his worst moments as a racing driver: a pair of badly buckled steering wheels. The first came from the Lotus 18 in which he left the road at Spa in 1960 when a wheel came off as the axle shaft broke, sending him into an earth bank, breaking both his legs and his nose and crushing several spinal vertebrae. On that occasion, to the world's astonishment and applause, he was back in the cockpit within seven weeks. The second steering wheel belonged to the Lotus 18/21 in which he crashed at Goodwood on 23 April 1962, a still unexplained incident which inflicted severe facial wounds, crushed his left cheekbone and displaced the eye socket, broke his left arm, left knee and left ankle, smashed his nose, put him into a coma for a month, left him paralysed down his left side for six months, and finished his career at the age of 32, with races and championships still to be won.

In front of him on his desk were two Collins Royal No. 25 diaries, each one three-quarters of an inch thick and bound in red cloth. In his forward-sloping hand, and usually in blue ink, Moss recorded on their pages the details of his life as a racing driver. Now he looked at one of them, dated 1954, and relived the first of his two visits to Pescara.

'On Thursday the 12th of August I went to Maserati in Modena and saw Orsi,' he said, reading from the pages. Omer Orsi, the son of the man who bought the company from the Maserati brothers, had been impressed by Moss's performance in his privately entered and green-painted 250F in the early months of 1954. Now he was proposing a semi-works contract. 'He offered me 50 per cent of the starting money and prize money when I used a factory car and 50 per cent plus 65,000 lire and half the insurance when I was in my own car. We got one and a half million lire to start, I think, which was quite good.' At about 1750 lire to the pound, that would mean roughly £850. 'After lunch I went into the factory. Then Pete Ayles, who was teaching me to fly, and I took off for Imola in a single-engined Cessna. I was trying to get the miles for my licence.' At Imola, at the circuit in the hills just outside the town, he tested a two-litre sports Maserati, the A6GCS model. 'Best time 2.11, Musso 2.09.' At 5.15pm, with a mechanic in the passenger's seat, he left Imola in the little Maserati and set off for Pescara, heading along the Via Emilia to Rimini before turning down the Adriatic coast. He arrived at 9.05pm, had dinner with Peter Collins, and was in bed at 12.45.

The following day, Friday the 13th, he rose at nine. The traffic had kept him awake, and probably also the late-night firework displays with which Pescara celebrated

Ferragosto. In the morning he went out in the sports Maserati and covered five laps of the unfamiliar circuit, after which he felt confident that he had committed its salient features to memory. At least one of those laps, at racing speed, was in company with a journalist, the highly knowledgeable Denis Jenkinson. In his own diary, Jenkinson recorded the experience with a single word: 'Terrific!' (Eighteen months later, when Moss was looking for someone who could navigate him round the course of the 1955 Mille Miglia, he remembered how Jenkinson, a former sidecar racer, had relished the experience, combining a complete absence of fear with an ability to appreciate what was going on around him; together they went on to win a famous victory, Jenkinson reading pace-notes from a roll of paper while Moss hurled their Mercedes 300SLR around Italy.) Later in the day Moss was approached by Signor Volpate of the Lancia sports car team, who had been sent to sign him to drive the team's 3.8-litre sports car in the Tourist Trophy. 'He said I could have the car and mechanics at Monza for five to seven days if I wished,' Moss recorded. 'Pretty surprising.' Flattering, he meant, but the offer was not taken up.

On the Saturday he was up at 7.50am and went to the circuit for the first of two practice sessions with his own Maserati 250F, which had been repainted red by the factory but was still attended by his own mechanics, Alf Francis and Tony Robinson. It was a hot day, eventually reaching 110 degrees, and Moss recorded the gear ratios, plug types and carburettor settings he had used. To start with, the car would only run on five of its six cylinders, thanks to a water leak, but with a new engine fitted he was timed at 10min 23sec, the fastest ever recorded at the circuit – albeit with two of the three pre-war chicanes removed – and 21 seconds ahead of the next quickest car, a Ferrari driven by Robert Manzon. 'Had lunch,' Moss wrote, 'and then we went to the garage and shopping before dinner.'

He was up at 7.15 on Sunday, and off to the circuit straight away. By 9.05, when the race began, it was already a scorching day. A bad start left him lying third, but he was in the lead by the time the cars flashed past the pits at the end of the first lap, and after three laps he had stretched his advantage to more than half a minute. But on the next lap 'Moss's bad-luck bogey', as journalists often called it, intervened and the gearbox suddenly lost its oil when a pipe broke. 'Fini,' he wrote. He could only watch as Luigi Musso led a clean sweep for Maserati, with Behra and Schell second and third. As ever at Pescara, the whole thing was over by lunchtime. In the afternoon he worked on his car with Francis and went for a swim. He had dinner at Jenkinson's hotel on the Via Milano, and they called in at the post-race dance. 'Dead loss,' Moss decided. 'Bed at 12.30.' In the morning he was off early with Pete Ayles in the little Cessna, flying to Rome, on to Florence and thence to Cannes, where he checked into the Hôtel Gray d'Albion, met friends and made plans for the following day's waterskiing.

By the time Moss returned to Pescara three years later he had become a star. In 1955 he won the Mille Miglia, the Targa Florio and, in front of an excited Aintree crowd, his first *grande épreuve*, all at the wheel of Mercedes cars. In 1956, leading the Maserati team, he had won the grands prix of Monaco and Italy, finishing as runner-up to Fangio in the championship for the second time in a row. But in

1957 he was able to realise his ambition of challenging for the championship in a British car: the Vanwall, with a chassis designed by a young genius, Colin Chapman.

Patriotic by nature, Moss had become obsessed with the idea after Enzo Ferrari had invited him to drive one of his cars at Bari in 1951. After he had dragged himself all the way down to the south-east of Italy, Ferrari casually reneged on the promise. Subsequently Moss tried his best with all sorts of half-baked British cars – the HWM, the Cooper-Alta, the G-type ERA – until it was necessary to own up and temporarily throw in his lot with Italian and German engineering.

Even when he signed his Vanwall contract, it was in the knowledge that the car he was leaving was nicer than the one he was going to. 'The Vanwall was no 250F, I'll tell you that,' he said. 'Aerodynamically it was pretty good, which helped at places like Monza, and the disc brakes were good, too, although I'd had those fitted to my Maser. The engine was good, once they'd sorted out a dreadful flat spot, but the gearbox was very difficult to synchronise and in general, being a typical Colin Chapman design, the car was not user-friendly. Chapman's designs may have been the best, but they were not easy to use. They were not constant cars, that was the trouble. They were prone to both oversteer and understeer, and they'd just switch from the one to the other. I don't know enough technically to be able to say how or why. No, the Vanwall may have beaten the 250F, but it was never a nicer car. It did what it was built for and won the world championship and so one can't really criticise it. But it was not a driver's car.'

Under his new contract, negotiated by his manager, Ken Gregory, with the team's owner, Tony Vandervell, he was to receive a retainer of £5000, paid in eight instalments; £500 in starting money for each round of the world championship and £400 for other races; and 60 per cent of prize money and bonuses. But the Vanwalls were not ready for the opening race of the world championship season in Argentina, so Vandervell agreed to loan him back to Maserati, for whom he would, in any case, be driving sports cars again that season. At the Buenos Aires autodrome he drove the new lightweight 250F alongside Fangio and Behra, but a problem with the throttle linkage delayed him and he could finish no higher than eighth. A win for Fangio seemed like the prelude to another season of success for the Argentinian maestro. Moss spent the first 10 weeks of the season on the other side of the Atlantic, taking part in various sports car races in Argentina, Cuba and the US. On the sunbaked airfield circuit at Sebring, teamed with Schell in the 12-hour race, he finished second.

When he finally eased himself over the high wrap-around screen of the Vanwall and into its spacious cockpit, his early experiences were mixed. On the road circuit at Syracuse he and Brooks led the Ferraris and Maseratis convincingly, only for broken fuel and water pipes to delay them. Moss made his way back through the field to finish third, while Brooks retired. At the Easter Goodwood meeting, facing the BRMs and Connaughts in the Glover Trophy, they were again dominant until stopped by minor breakages. Their speed was beyond doubt, but a frustrated Vandervell was urging his engineers to examine the components that were proving fragile and to modify or replace them. A new type of high-pressure rubber pipe, for example, was used on the fuel injection system after breakages in the first two races, caused by vibration. After intensive work on the cars at

Acton, Moss took pole position at Monaco and was leading the race until a mistake at the chicane on the third lap sent him into the barriers, taking the Ferraris of Hawthorn and Collins with him. Fangio won the race at a canter, ahead of Brooks.

After that came the Nürburgring 1000kms sports car race, where Moss and Fangio lost a wheel on their Maserati, and Le Mans, to which he took Katie Molson, his fiancée. This was a nostalgic trip, since it was where they had met a year earlier, when Moss spotted a gamine girl on the other side of the track and, using hand gestures, arranged a rendezvous at the entrance to the pits. In 1957, however, she had to sit and watch while he endured an unhappy race at the wheel of a special coupé-bodied Maserati 450S. At Moss's behest, the body had been commissioned from Frank Costin, who had been brought in by Chapman to design the Vanwall's bodywork. Maserati grudgingly arranged for it to be built by Zagato, the celebrated Italian coachbuilder noted for the voluptuous beauty of their own designs. Such was Zagato's resentment at being required to execute the blueprint of an English designer, however, that the work was studiously botched. Costin's careful aerodynamic calculations were thrown out of kilter, particularly when the air intakes and vents were cut in the wrong places, meaning that the engine would not deliver maximum power and the cabin was permanently filled with superheated fumes. It was, in the end, a strong candidate for nomination as the worst car Moss ever drove.

After that dismal experience, a few days with Katie on the Côte d'Azur seemed the ideal medicine. At Juan les Pins and La Napoule they waterskied, went dancing at the Whisky A Go-Go, won 4000 francs at the casino and watched the beautiful people of the era, including Lord and Lady Docker, gossip-column regulars famous for owning a Rolls-Royce with solid-gold door handles. It was while Moss was practising 360-degree turnarounds on a monoski that a jet of salt water forced itself up his nasal passages. In the early hours of Wednesday, 3 July, the day he was scheduled to travel to Rouen for the grand prix, he was suddenly in such pain that he needed injections.

On the flight to Paris he was accompanied by Herbert Mackay-Fraser, the 29-year-old Connecticut-born son of the owner of a Brazilian coffee plantation. Mackay-Fraser had arrived in Europe two years earlier and showed such immediate promise at the wheel of his own Ferrari sports car that Colin Chapman took him into the Lotus team in 1956. For the following year he signed up with the BRM team, alongside Ron Flockhart, while continuing to drive for Lotus in sports car races.

On arrival in Paris, Mackay-Fraser waved farewell and set off for Rouen, while Moss was taken to a local hospital where, over the course of the next three days, he was given pills and lumbar injections to ease the continuing pain in his sinuses. On the Saturday the doctors said he could leave, but the injections meant he could not drive. He was driven to Deauville, then flown to Croydon, and taken by ambulance to the London Clinic, where he stayed for six days while doctors took X-rays and blood tests and drained his antrum twice, drilling through the septum. He was released on Friday the 12th, and was recovering at home when he heard the news that Mackay-Fraser had been killed in the Formula Two race at Rheims, becoming the first man to die at the wheel of a works Lotus. The following Thursday, fully recovered, but having missed the *grande épreuve* at Rouen and the non-championship race at Rheims, Moss was on his way to Liverpool, preparing to race.

This was the second time the British Grand Prix had been held around the perimeter road at Aintree racecourse, where the start took place in front of grandstands more familiar from pictures of the Grand National. For the first time, three Vanwalls were entered. Moss and Brooks were returning, the latter still recovering from a heavy crash at Le Mans a month earlier. Now they were joined by Stuart Lewis-Evans, who had stepped willingly into the breach for the two races in France and had impressed Vandervell and the team's manager, David Yorke, with his speed and competence.

Once again Moss started from pole position, with Brooks on the outside of the front row and Behra's Maserati between them. Moss led from the start, but after 21 laps he was in the pits with an incurable misfire. The tiring Brooks, who had dropped down to sixth place, was called in at the end of lap 27 and was lifted from his healthy car by the mechanics before Moss jumped in to begin the chase. Having fallen to ninth place after the handover, for the remaining 63 of the 90 laps he hunted down one opponent after another. Overtaking Fangio on lap 34, Musso on lap 40, Collins on lap 46 and Lewis-Evans on lap 69, he was up to third place behind Behra's Maserati and Hawthorn's Ferrari when, with 20 laps to go, luck finally turned his and Vanwall's way. Behra's clutch exploded, dropping shards of metal on to the track. As Hawthorn went by the Frenchman's stricken 250F and into the lead, one of the Ferrari's wheels ran over the debris and punctured a tyre, forcing the Englishman to head straight for the pits. Now Moss was in the lead, ahead of Lewis-Evans in second place and with sufficient margin to allow him a precautionary refuelling stop. Although Lewis-Evans dropped back to seventh place with a broken throttle linkage, the Aintree crowd were delighted to acclaim the green car which had finally vanquished the red hordes in a world championship race.

Was Moss's exercise of his *droit de seigneur* a cause of resentment inside the team? 'To an extent,' he said. 'It was very difficult to exercise and it caused a lot of friction. If my car blew up, they had to give me another one. We had a good team, the strongest there was. I think Tony was the best unknown driver there ever was, if you know what I mean. I have great respect for his ability. His career was cut short when he got married to Pina. But he was very quick, as was Stuart Lewis-Evans. If you looked at the other teams, they had one driver who was bloody good and the other two weren't close. We were all fairly close.'

The euphoria did not last long. Two weeks later at the Nürburgring the Vanwall suspension proved totally unsuited to the long, undulating circuit in the Eifel mountains. Fangio won the German Grand Prix with one of the most celebrated and spectacular drives of his career, earning the nine points – eight for a win, one for the fastest lap during the race – that gave him his fifth championship, with two rounds of the series still to go. Meanwhile Moss bumped and bounced his way to a dismal fifth, a nauseous Brooks was ninth, Lewis-Evans crashed, and the team wondered whether Aintree had been a mirage.

After a trip to Sweden with the Maserati sports car team, Moss returned to London and prepared to head south to

Pescara with his father. Alfred Moss was a London dentist who had raced before the war and, after putting up initial token opposition, had supported his son's early career. 'My father came to most of the races, and my mother quite a lot, too,' Moss said. 'I suppose I bounced things off my father. He and Ken Gregory, my manager, had ordered the Maserati without my knowledge in 1953, having been to see Alfred Neubauer at Mercedes, who told them, "Well, we've seen him driving a lot of crap. We need to see him in a better environment, to see if he can handle it." My father was quite a good businessman. He was a dentist by profession, but he'd done other things. The Morrison Shelter, which people used during the war, was his invention, although it was named after a politician. And he had raced, of course. He'd done quite a lot of things. When I started, he said, "No way are you going to drive. You can't make a living at that." Which, of course, you couldn't, then. I enjoyed having him around.' Didn't it cramp the style of a highly libidinous young man? 'Not at all. He'd go to bed.'

Responsible, under the terms of the Vanwall deal, for his own travel and accommodation expenses, Moss was budget-conscious to a degree that others sometimes found amusing. Like his insistence on physical fitness, systematic fiscal prudence was part of a highly organised approach to his working life, an attitude that was to make him the best-paid driver of his time and which would form a bridge between the amateur ethos, still visible in the way Collins or Hawthorn went about their lives, and the more rigorous approach of a coming generation of professionals.

Moss and his father would seldom stay in the same hotel as the team management and the other drivers. 'Any hotel that I would have gone to anywhere would have been one of the cheaper ones,' he said. In Monaco, for instance, he had a regular 20 per cent discount deal with the Metropole Hotel, just down the track from the Casino square. ('Moss was always thrifty in his choice of hotel and food,' his friend Bernard Cahier remembered, 'and his father was worse. When he got married to Katie Molson, she liked to have wine with a meal. His father objected: too expensive.')

The day before leaving for Pescara he kept an appointment with Godfrey Smith of the *Sunday Times* and appeared that night on *Sportsview*, BBC TV's midweek sports magazine programme. He got to bed at 2.15am and was up again at 7am to catch a plane from London airport. He was allowed into the cockpit for both the take-off and the landing into Rome, from where he picked up the Fiat hire car and drove his father down to Pescara, a journey of three and a half hours on a road he knew well from the Mille Miglia, albeit travelling in the opposite direction. When they arrived he took the Fiat around the circuit, reacquainting himself with its geography. On one of the laps his passenger was Gregor Grant, editor and grand prix correspondent of *Autosport*.

Moss quickly remembered how much he liked the circuit. By this time he had taken part in many road races in Italy and France, and it was the kind of racing he most enjoyed. 'I'd raced at Lake Garda, Périgueux, Les Sables d'Olonne and Bordeaux, lots of places.' He could also have mentioned Aix les Bains, Berne, Marseille, San Remo, Bari, Naples, Mons, Caen or Castelfusano. 'Pescara was quite a tiring circuit, with the heat, but as a driver you got a tremendous amount of fulfilment from it. The races we had at Silverstone and Goodwood and so on were never the same sort of thing.'

4

The Road

'I think part of the attraction of motor racing was the danger,' Stirling Moss said. 'That was part of the reason you wanted to do it.' Looking back from the vantage point of an age in which death is no longer a regular and inescapable feature of motor racing, the risks taken by the men of Moss's generation seem increasingly hard to comprehend. In Moss's day the cars were still built to suit the tracks, which were based on natural topographical features: the hilly countryside lying between villages, for example, or the narrow, winding streets of a seaside town. Nowadays the new grand prix circuits, with their profusion of safety features, are located on waste land and designed to suit the cars. Usually created by the same architect, they are virtually interchangeable and have no more to do with their immediate surroundings than the layout of a Scalextric track has to do with the furniture in a boy's bedroom. However much skill and courage Michael Schumacher may possess, his mastery of modern circuit racing bears almost no resemblance to the qualities needed to prevail in races run over public roads. Which is not to say, of course, that Schumacher would necessarily have been unable to compete with the giants of earlier eras on their terms, any more than it is to suggest that Moss would have failed to adapt to the world of traction control, automatic gearboxes and split-second pitstop routines. But the hugely increased role played by technology, particularly since computers came along, has reduced both the degree to which the driver can be seen to be driving the car and, just as important, the scope for his errors to influence the pattern of events. In the course of that evolution, perhaps inevitably, grand prix racing has gradually forfeited much of its human appeal.

The automobile was still a new invention when motor racing began in the last decade of the nineteenth century. The earliest races were time trials, attracting competitors with vehicles powered by a variety of sources. By 1899, however, the petrol engine had more or less won the day, and that year the entrants in the Paris to Bordeaux race enjoyed an innovation: instead of setting off at timed intervals, they all started at once, and the first to cross the finish line would be declared the winner.

Although the biggest of the pioneering events were staged – or at least started – in France, Italy's first motor race had been held in 1895, over the road from Turin to Asti and back. A distance of 58 miles, it was covered by the winner, Simone Federman in a Daimler omnibus, at an average speed of 15.5mph. Enthusiasm for road racing spread: only in Britain and Germany was it deemed to be so dangerous that laws were passed to prohibit it. Elsewhere all sorts of events proliferated: races from Marseille to Nice, from Paris to Dieppe, from Paris to Amsterdam and back, from Padua to Treviso and back, from Paris to Toulouse, Nice–Salon–Nice, and from Paris to Vienna. In the United States, the first road race took place on Long Island in 1900. A year later the death of a small boy hit by a car during the Paris–Berlin race led to a temporary ban on events held on the open roads of France, and racing began to move to closed circuits at which, notionally at least, some control could be exercised over competitors and spectators.

Sometimes these circuits were specialised tracks. More often they were normal roads closed by arrangement with local authorities, who could see the publicity value of such extraordinary events. In Belgium, the roads around Bastogne provided a 53-mile layout called the Circuit des Ardennes, which attracted 49 starters to a six-lap race in 1902. Two years later Count Vincenzo Florio inaugurated his Coppa Florio over a 104-mile loop outside Brescia. Britain got round its ban by holding races in the Gordon Bennett series over road circuits in Ireland and on the Isle of Man. In 1904 the leading lights of France and Italy took ship to the US, where they met their American counterparts in a competition for the Vanderbilt Cup on the Long Island track.

In 1906 the future shape of motor racing emerged when the Auto Club de France organised a race called simply Le Grand Prix, a two-day event of 769 miles over 12 laps of a circuit outside the town of Le Mans, open to cars with a maximum weight of a thousand kilograms. An over-subscribed entry was whittled down to ten teams from France, two from Italy and one from Germany. Significantly, the town paid the ACF a fee for the right to hold the race, and invested heavily in laying new road surfaces, bypassing villages, creating a paddock area and building grandstands. The commercial appeal of grand prix racing had been established. François Szisz won the race in a Renault fitted with a three-speed gearbox, shaft drive and detachable wheel rims, ahead of Felice Nazzarro's Fiat. That same year Count Florio moved his race to his native Sicily, where the rechristened Targa Florio was held on a 92-mile circuit around the bandit-infested mountain roads.

The Targa Florio was an immediate success; meanwhile Dieppe outbid Le Mans for the second and third editions of the Grand Prix. Other races were organised all over France and Italy: it was to the Circuito di Bologna that the 10-year-old Enzo Ferrari was taken by his father in 1908, to see Nazzarro and Vincenzo Lancia duelling in their Fiats over the dusty roads. But racing over public roads had received a challenge in 1907, when H. F. Locke-King commissioned a track to be built at Brooklands, his estate in Surrey, to the south-west of London. A concrete speed-oval, with a wall-of-death banking at either end, its existence was announced by S. F. Edge's successful attempt on the 24-hour distance record, covering 1581 miles in his Napier at an average of 65.9mph. Across the Atlantic, the equally imposing Indianapolis Motor Speedway, two and a half miles long, was opened in 1909. Its inaugural race was a two-lap sprint; the famous 500-mile race was held for the first time two years later. Similar ventures included the vast board track at Playa del Rey in Beverly Hills, California (1910), a combined road and track circuit in the royal park at Monza, outside Milan (1922), and similar layouts at Linas–Montlhéry, south-east of Paris, and Miramas, near Marseille (both 1925).

Now France could no longer claim the name 'Grand Prix' as its sole property. The Americans had been the first to ride the bandwagon, holding the Grand Prize of the Automobile

Club of America in Savannah, Georgia, in 1908. After the First World War the ACF's event became the French Grand Prix, held successively at Dieppe, Amiens, Lyons, Le Mans and Montlhéry. The British Grand Prix was staged at Brooklands, and later over the private circuit at Donington Park in the East Midlands. Monza hosted the Italian Grand Prix. And in Germany, as part of a project to reduce unemployment, a circuit was built around the Eifel mountains; it would attempt, with great success, to mimic the challenges of the great open-road circuits. The Nürburgring, as it was called, had no towns or villages to be negotiated, and no unmade roads or lurking bandits, but it did have 14.7 miles of narrow and endlessly undulating tarmac, featuring no fewer than 174 corners and countless changes of camber and gradient bordered by hedges and ditches.

Gradually the length of the open-road circuits was coming down. Amiens measured 23.5 miles, the revised Le Mans 10.75, Strasbourg 13.4, Tours 14.1, Lyons 14.3, and the new circuit at Spa-Francorchamps, a successor to the Circuit des Ardennes, a mere 8.76. These dimensions enabled some sort of control to be retained in a massed-start race, while providing the conditions of authentic motoring. By contrast the artificial circuits of Monza and Montlhéry measured 6.2 and 7.7 miles, and Brooklands a tiny 2.8 miles. And now, too, there were races around the streets of towns: Monaco, Pau, Turin, San Remo, Rome, Naples, where hoteliers and shopkeepers started to recognise the commercial benefits to be derived from an influx of spectators.

So it went on through the 1920s and into the 1930s, from battles between Bugattis and Alfa Romeos to a golden age witnessing the battles between Mercedes-Benz and Auto

Union, high-technology cars of enormous power with a generation of remarkable drivers at the wheel. They raced on a combination of artificial parkland tracks, true road courses, and the occasional speed bowl. Sports cars were tested in the Targa Florio and the Mille Miglia, the historic time trials around the roads of Sicily and mainland Italy, and in the 24 Hours of Le Mans, where a course created from public roads was gradually being adapted to suit the needs of speed and safety.

In South America, the evolution of the sport was tending strongly in the direction of open-road time trials. Juan Manuel Fangio made his name in the great transcontinental road races, driving a stripped-down Chevrolet coupé to victory in the Gran Premio del Norte and the Argentine 1000-mile race in 1940, at the age of 29. These were endlessly gruelling races over often impossibly inhospitable terrain, with unmade surfaces and sheer drops, in which stages across the Altiplano brought on altitude sickness relieved only by chewing coca leaves. To ward off weariness, there were specially formulated pills. No driver could hope to learn these roads: the art of improvisation was as essential as a basic ruggedness of spirit.

In Britain, by contrast, the end of the Second World War brought an evolutionary leap in the opposite direction. Before the war, British motor sport had been an insular and class-ridden affair. Meetings at Brooklands were advertised with a famous slogan: 'The right crowd, and no crowding.' It might have been Ascot or Henley. The war helped break that down. Fighter squadrons, for instance, had originally been composed largely of Oxbridge men, but the rate of fatalities necessitated the introduction of pilots from a broader social spectrum, including a number of men who had begun their RAF life as ground crew. British life had begun the gradual and often painful process of democratisation, and motor racing would soon show its effects.

After demobilisation, there were plenty of young men looking for excitement, some of whom had learnt mechanical skills and were comfortable with spanners, spark plugs and even blueprints. There were also plenty of even younger men who had just missed out on active service but had been brought up on inspiring tales of the heroism of Spitfire and Hurricane pilots in the Battle of Britain, and were looking for some similar form of self-expression, preferably involving physical risk. Others of a more technical nature felt, whether consciously or not, that they were part of a tradition exemplified by Sidney Camm and R. J. Mitchell, the designers of the Hurricane and the Spitfire respectively, and by the ingenious Barnes-Wallis, the inventor of the 'bouncing bomb'. Just as significant, there was also a profusion of decommissioned airfields scattered around the country, waiting to be exploited. The result of this combination of ambition, available facilities, mechanical inquisitiveness and post-war austerity was the birth of the British club racing scene, exemplified by the category which became known as Formula Three. Here tiny rear-engined cars powered by 500cc motorcycle engines raced on circuits formed from the perimeter runways of old airfields, using straw bales and oil cans as markers, and perhaps an old control tower as a clubhouse.

The designers produced by this era were responsible for creating the modern racing car. They began by stripping down small family saloons, often the ubiquitous Austin Seven or Ford Popular, and using the components to create primitive racing cars. The same thing had happened in Italy, where garages were full of small Fiats being turned into competition machines. But whereas in Italy the resulting specials would race over road courses which placed a premium on strength and durability, in Britain the smooth airfield circuits encouraged the new generation of designers to built very light cars with sensitive steering and independent suspension. And when John Cooper put the motorcycle engine of his first car behind the driver, gradually others came to see the sense of such an arrangement. What had appeared to be an eccentricity when the pre-war Auto Union emerged from the pen of Dr Ferdinand Porsche, eventually came to seem the obvious way of doing things, although the sport's grandee constructors, notably Enzo Ferrari, took some years to be convinced. When Colin Chapman built lightness into his Lotus cars, shaving away every bit of excess weight from the components (and sometimes, regrettably, an amount of weight that proved to have been not excessive but integral), they gained such an obvious advantage that the rest had to follow suit.

This revolution, which began at the very roots of the sport, at the lowest level of competition, had barely begun to make itself felt in the higher echelons when 16 cars were pushed on to the grid in Pescara in August 1957. But its pre-echoes were unmistakable.

5

Brooks

Along the hallway of Tony and Pina Brooks's apartment, part of a vast Surrey mansion built for a Belgian baronet a hundred years ago, are hung a series of enlarged photographs of motor races, depicting significant moments from Tony Brooks's time as one of the world's finest racing drivers. Here he is cresting the Burnenville rise at Spa, on his way to victory with the Vanwall in the spring of 1958. And there, a year later, he can be seen rounding the Parabolica at Monza during a practice session in his Ferrari, the day before his clutch burned out on the line, costing him a very good chance of winning the world championship; instead he finished as runner-up to Jack Brabham, missing immortality by a whisker.

The display is wonderfully evocative. 'My wife's idea,' he said, gently dismissing any notion of self-aggrandisement while leading his visitor away down the corridor and into elegantly furnished rooms from which virtually all signs of his career as a racing driver have been expunged.

The first time Charles Anthony Standish Brooks sat in a Formula One car was in Sicily on the morning of 23 October

1955, during practice day for the Gran Premio di Siracusa, a non-championship race. Just over 24 hours later he would become the first British driver to win a foreign grand prix in a British car since 1924, when Sir Henry Segrave drove a Sunbeam to victory in San Sebastian.

Then aged 23, Brooks was a Manchester dental student whose performances in a Frazer-Nash and a Formula Two Connaught had impressed the managements of the Aston Martin sports car team and the Connaught grand prix outfit. Earlier in the season he had competed in his first two road races, driving the Frazer-Nash in the Tourist Trophy at Dundrod in Ireland and an Aston at Le Mans. Syracuse, however, was something different. 'It was very much a road circuit, just ordinary roads closed for the occasion with brick walls round most of it, and quite rough, as Sicilian roads were in those days,' he said. 'It was a bit of a baptism of fire, I guess you could call it.'

He had missed the first of two days of practice over the 3.4-mile circuit, which featured a couple of level crossings. The team's converted AEC single-decker buses had departed on schedule from the Connaught garage at Send, near Guildford in Surrey, but arrived at the circuit 24 hours late. 'They had a tremendous job getting down there, over umpteen mountain passes. Going round the hairpins it was back-forwards, back-forwards, back-forwards. They had terrible trouble with the brakes, and the net result was that they only arrived on the Saturday morning, the day before the race.'

Brooks had driven a sports Connaught at Aintree during the British Grand Prix meeting, finishing second in his supporting race, but was astonished to be invited to join the team for a proper grand prix. 'I think the explanation is that they couldn't find anybody else,' he said. 'It was way past the end of the season, and Connaught didn't have a very good reputation. Sicily was a long way away in '55. It seemed like the other end of the world. You couldn't even fly direct. You had to fly to Rome, then from Rome to Catania. I don't think anybody else was interested, frankly. The Connaught was unreliable, it wasn't competitive, so who wanted to do it? I think it was as simple as that. They paid my expenses and a share of the starting money.'

In the penultimate year of his course of studies to qualify as a dentist, and only two months away from a set of serious professional exams, Brooks used the plane journeys to catch up with his studies. 'You had to pass your exams every year, otherwise you didn't go forward to the next lot,' he said. 'If you failed the same exams twice, you were out. And it probably took my mind off what I'd gone and done.'

He was surprised to win the 70-lap race; now he is amazed at what he achieved. 'That's the understatement of the day, although it didn't strike me at the time. I enjoyed driving, I just went there to do a job, and that was it. I was obviously very pleased because it was against a full works Maserati team, which, after Mercedes, was the most competitive at the time. Ferrari were really out of it in '55. There were seven Maseratis, I think, three or four works cars with Musso and Villoresi and Schell, and Roy [Salvadori] with his Maserati.' So nonplussed were the Italians that the race director, Renzo Castagneto, who had been one of the founders of the Mille Miglia, insisted on having the Connaught's engine measured because, in the words of *Motor Sport*'s correspondent, 'He felt that the Italian newspapers would never believe it possible for the whole Maserati team to be beaten by an unknown car and driver.'

Unknown, he added, to the Italian public: 'not unknown to British enthusiasts, for Brooks has been a visible "natural driver" since he first appeared on a racing circuit.' The engine turned out to be perfectly legal.

Brooks enjoyed every aspect of the experience. The proximity of walls, ditches, trees and telegraph poles did not disturb him. 'I never aimed to go off the road. It is road racing, after all. An awful lot of people can drive well when they know they can go off the road and not hurt themselves. It's not the same challenge. That's what's wrong today. There's just no comparison with the sport in our day. I'm not against the idea of safety. But in becoming so safe, it's become a totally different sport. It's like comparing a tightrope walker in a circus with a safety net with a tightrope walker crossing a ravine, above a great big drop. I think that's a totally valid comparison.'

The attitude to risk is at the root of the change, he said. 'It's a sociological factor. You're not supposed to risk your life at all these days. It's more than fifty years, thank goodness, since we've been involved in what you might call a proper war, so people no longer understand that life can involve a high degree of risk. Think about what happened in London during the Blitz. There were bombs raining down constantly, every day you could be killed, and people took it in their stride. "It could happen," they thought, "but it probably won't." Now people think it's abhorrent to do anything that involves risk.'

Death was a common occurrence in grand prix racing at the time Brooks reached the top. 'When someone died we were very sad and we went to their funeral and it hurt, but if it upset you deeply you should retire. If you start to think you're in danger of killing yourself, you shouldn't continue.

I personally was blessed with a fair degree of natural ability and I never had to psych myself up to produce a good time. I never forced myself to go beyond my natural speed, and I was fortunate that my natural speed was fast enough to be competitive and to win races. But I never went into a race thinking, "I might kill myself today." There was always a risk that you'd come round a corner and there'd be oil on the track or a car in the way and you'd have an accident through no fault of your own, but apart from that I would never have been considering the idea that I was going to hurt myself, still less kill myself. If another driver's death had undermined my belief in my ability to drive safely, I would have stopped. But it didn't. I had two big accidents in my career, and neither was due to a misjudgement. To me, road racing is the only form of racing. Motor racing started with races from city to city, and the further you get away from that, the further you're getting away from the spirit of grand prix racing.'

The historic win in Sicily turned out to be of no lasting benefit to Connaught, whose finances were already precarious. Less than two years later Bernie Ecclestone, a Kent car dealer with ambitions to enter grand prix racing, bought a couple of their cars at a knock-down price. He was laying plans to start a new team for his protégé Stuart Lewis-Evans, whose potential had become obvious in Formula Three races at Brands Hatch, where Ecclestone himself had raced similar cars a few years earlier against Lewis-Evans's father.

But Syracuse helped promote Brooks's reputation for speed and consistency, and at the start of 1956 he joined Mike Hawthorn in the BRM grand prix team. It was hardly an auspicious time: the British Racing Motors operation was slowly recovering from the disastrous failure of the company's sophisticated 1.5-litre supercharged car, built to the old Formula One regulations with the aid of public subscription. 'Their engineering standards were quite high but they had no idea of how to test and develop the car,' Brooks said. 'With development, the car they built in '56 could have been a grand prix winner. It was very light and it went like a rocket. But it was totally lethal to drive, and I use the term advisedly. If you didn't take a corner in a geometrical fashion, like a bicycle does, you were off.'

His distrust of the car and the team was confirmed when he survived a spectacular crash during the British Grand Prix at Silverstone. 'The throttle cable broke during the race, so I pulled off at Stowe and lashed it up,' he said. 'Then it was repaired, if you can call it that, at the pits, and I set off again. I'd been taking Abbey Curve flat, which in the BRM means that I must have been mental. And on the first lap after the pit stop I noticed that the throttle was a little bit sticky.' While he had been sitting in the pits, however, more rubber and oil had gone on to the surface of the curve, making it more slippery, which meant that he needed to lift off the throttle. But when he lifted, nothing happened. The throttle had stuck again. Entering the corner too fast, he ran wide on to the grass. 'With any respectable grand prix car, you'd have been able to ease it gradually back on to the track. But that car took control, spun across the track, hit the bank, turned over, threw me out, and then did the decent thing and set itself on fire.' It also broke Brooks's jaw.

His disappointment with the BRM was assuaged by a meeting with a young Italian woman at the Rouen sports car race that summer. Pina Resegotti, a student of modern languages, was on her way from her home in Milan to finish her thesis at the British Museum in London; she had broken the journey to stay with a friend who happened to be the daughter of the race organiser. Her fluency in French, English and Spanish as well as her native language brought an invitation to act as an interpreter, but soon after meeting her that weekend Brooks added a *Teach Yourself Italian* textbook to his pile of study material. 'I'd been in the habit of studying every night for as long as I could remember,' he said, 'so I used that habit to teach myself Italian, and I saw her again in England when she came over. Her father was a substantial farmer outside Milan, near Pavia – he kept half Milan alive during the war and afterwards.'

Not wanting to waste his years of study, Brooks began to practise dentistry at the Turner Dental School in Manchester, where he had qualified in December 1956. 'I stayed there because there was much more flexibility to getting time off. Eventually I felt I was beginning to abuse their goodwill, because I was getting into a situation where I was away more than I was there. And they'd been so good. So I practised for a period before I packed it in.' Unlike most of his fellow drivers, he had never accepted an invitation to spend the winter racing in Australia and New Zealand. 'I had this guilt complex. I felt I owed it to the hospital to prove my services to them. One makes mistakes in life, and that was one of mine.' But in November, a few weeks before his final exams, the call came to attend at a test session run by the Vanwall team at Oulton Park, the nearest circuit to his home in Manchester. He had been impressed with what he had seen of Tony Vandervell's latest car, and the fact that Stirling Moss had shown enough faith in the

Vanwall's potential to sign up also impressed him. He was happy to join as Moss's number two.

'Oulton was a tough circuit,' he said, 'and I still hadn't really got a name. I'd just had a disastrous season with BRM. I think I had only raced in one grand prix, in which I nearly managed to kill myself with that stuck throttle. They withdrew from all the other races. So I'd only got Syracuse to my credit. I think it was more a question of them testing me than of me testing the car.'

His basic retainer for the season was around £2000, supplemented by 50 per cent of starting money and prize money, and 60 per cent of the small bonuses paid by equipment manufacturers who used Vanwall's successes to publicise the quality of their products, including BP (petrol), KLG (spark plugs), Ferodo (disc brakes), Valspar (bodywork paint) and Hepworth and Grandage (Hepolite pistons). From his home at 8 Park Lane, Dukinfield, Cheshire, Brooks wrote to Vandervell on 21 February 1957, a few days before his 25th birthday: 'Dear Mr Vandervell, Many thanks for your letter and cheque for £500. I also hope that the period I drive for you will prove to be a happy one, and that your great efforts will be rewarded during the coming season. Yours sincerely, Tony Brooks.'

By contrast with the endless pre-season testing that would become part of the normal *modus operandi* adopted by Formula One teams of later generations, Brooks and the Vanwall hardly had an opportunity to get to know each other before they were off to the races. They missed the first race of the 1957 season, in Argentina, because the cars were not ready in time – something that happened quite a lot in those days, before Bernie Ecclestone's television deals stipulated the attendance of every team at all the races.

'That day at Oulton Park was the only test I did with them,' Brooks said. 'I think we went to the Easter meeting at Goodwood, but I was certainly not very familiar with the car when we arrived in Monaco for the first grand prix.'

After a season with BRM, he was relieved to discover that higher standards were in operation at Tony Vandervell's factory. Like all those who raced the Vanwall, however, he had reservations about the actual experience of driving the car, in particular its refusal to take corners in the sort of four-wheel drift perfected by Fangio and Moss. 'The Vanwall was a car that didn't particularly like drifting. It was the complete opposite of a car like the 250F Maserati. The Vanwall's basic tendency was to understeer. It was a very solid car in a mechanical sense, and you would know where you were with it, but it wasn't forgiving in the way a 250F was. You had to be very precise to get the best out of it. Virtually everybody else who tried it said the same thing. When Phil Hill and Dan Gurney tried it in a demonstration at Laguna Seca 10 years or so ago, that was enough to frighten them. But I'm not knocking it. It delivered the goods. It was a winner.'

After Moss had crashed on the fourth lap at Monaco, taking the Ferraris of Hawthorn and Collins with him, Brooks overcame the loss of his clutch after five of the scheduled 100 laps and finished a fine second to Fangio. By the end, after around 2400 clutchless gear-changes, the palm of his hand was like a piece of raw steak. 'It must have been a pretty strong gearbox – although it was also very heavy and ponderous, with a very long travel. Maybe if it hadn't been so heavy and strong I wouldn't have finished the race. And you don't need an excuse for finishing second to Fangio, do you?'

The cancellation of the Dutch and Belgian rounds of the world championship meant a long gap before the Vanwalls would be seen again. The drivers, however, were kept busy with sports car races, and at Le Mans on 23 June the shape of Brooks's season was abruptly modified. He was sharing a works Aston Martin with Noel Cunningham-Reid, and they were holding second place at three o'clock in the morning when his co-driver came into the pits with the gearbox stuck in fourth gear. Brooks had experienced the same problem in the car's previous race, where he had managed to free it. 'So I took over from Noel and I thought, well, the sooner I get this out of fourth gear the better, because with more than 12 hours to go we're just going to drop further and further down the field. Le Mans is a pretty boring race anyway, and to just sit there losing places all the time didn't appeal.

'On the third corner, between the Esses and Tertre Rouge, I was busy accelerating hard to put the load on the gearbox and suddenly taking my foot off to reduce the loading while pulling the lever to try and free it, when I did what learners are told not to do in their first driving lesson – I was looking down at the gear lever. I suddenly looked up and saw I was past my braking point. That was mistake number one. Mistake number two was that I almost got round the corner – if I'd gone straight on, I'd have hit the bank with a bit of a thump and that would have been the end of it. Instead I almost got round it by putting the car into a drift, but the idiots had put a sand-bank right to the edge of the road, and in almost getting round it, because I still had a lot of forward motion, I started edging up the bank. The car ran up the bank and flipped over and trapped me underneath.

'It was in the pitch dark at three o'clock in the morning, and it was past the apex of the corner, so I was aware that no one would realise there was a car in the way and that, more importantly, I was trapped underneath it. The question was whether I was going to be run over or incinerated, because cars in those days had a nasty habit of catching fire. I never lost consciousness. It's probably better that you do on such occasions. I was lying there waiting for the inevitable. So I was very fortunate that Umberto Maglioli came along in his Porsche and, being a gentleman, knocked the car off me instead of running over me, putting himself out of the race, too. I was extremely lucky. I managed to get up and scramble to the side of the road. But it was a genuinely heavy car and I had a great big hole in my right side, so big you could almost put your fist into it, and multiple abrasions and so on.'

After four or five days in a local hospital he was flown back to Britain in the private De Havilland Dove of David Brown, the owner of Aston Martin. No bones had been broken, but the cuts and bruises were severe. He missed the grand prix at Rouen and the non-championship race at Rheims, but within four weeks he was driving himself to Aintree. 'That was the first time I'd driven a car of any kind since the accident. I'd been pretty beaten up. Today I would never have been allowed to compete, but I conned them into letting me race.' His wounds were still healing, and he asked the mechanics to line the cockpit with soft rubber sheets. Amazingly, he put up the third fastest practice time, but completing a full race distance was another matter. 'It was understood that I would try and keep the car as high up the field as possible and that Stirling or Stuart would have it if they had trouble with their car, which is how it worked out.'

Moss took the chequered flag at Aintree, but Brooks shared in the champagne and the glory. The prize money – the first prize of 2500 guineas plus another £500 offered to the first British car to finish – was divided according to the number of laps each had driven.

'It was the only reason I ever handed over to Stirling,' Brooks remembered. 'Sometimes I was quicker than him and sometimes he was quicker than me. As it turned out, Stirling did a brilliant drive, although Behra and Mike [Hawthorn] fell on their own swords to a certain degree.' Had he stayed in the car, would he have won? 'That's a $50,000 question. If only . . . As it transpired, it didn't require a flat-out effort to win. But that's with 20–20 hindsight. We didn't know how it would pan out. We didn't know our two main competitors would have problems. I never look back. Not in rancour, anyway.'

As ever, Brooks took a gentlemanly view of Moss's status. 'The team spirit at Vanwall was very good, very strong, and Stirling was quite clearly number one. He had the choice of cars and he had the choice of engines. The only thing is that David Yorke tended to limit my practice once I'd got a respectable time, because if I did a quicker time than Stirling, which did happen, Stirling would grind round until he'd beaten it. He'd try my car. Sometimes he'd have my chassis and his engine, or vice versa. I was messed about a bit in that respect, and it did make life difficult on occasion. I think I started the odd race in a car I hadn't actually driven in practice, and in those days there were big differences between the chassis. Today they're produced with such fine scientific precision that you get into the spare car and it's identical to your race car. Not so then, not at all. I accepted it. I think it was sometimes counter-productive, though. When I was number one with Ferrari, I never took anyone else's car. I preferred to stay with the same car and try to really get it sorted and concentrate on getting a good lap time. The more you mess about, the more your objectives become non-focused. But I never had a cross word with Stirling because I knew he was entitled to do what he did. I never, ever complained because if I didn't like it, I shouldn't have signed on.'

He had still not fully recovered from the Le Mans accident when the drivers discovered that the car was a disaster around the Nürburgring. 'There was I, still with bandages all over the place, and the last thing I wanted was a rough ride. To say I got one is an understatement. The suspension was absolutely murderous. It was all a question of springs and shock absorbers. I don't think they had the right spring rates. I can only think they hadn't brought along the right equipment. And if you've got problems at the Nürburgring, because it's such a long lap, around ten minutes, it's not as easy to solve the problem in practice as it is where it's a two-minute lap. I got so badly beaten up in the race that I was physically sick in the cockpit during the last few laps. But I felt it was my duty to finish, although there was nothing I wanted more than to come in and park it.'

The race became famous as the setting for the greatest drive of Fangio's career, in which, after a pit stop, he continually broke the lap record by vast amounts during his successful chase of Hawthorn and Collins. Not that Brooks saw much of it. 'I suppose Fangio must have lapped me. I

Tony Vandervell (left, in Panama hat) with his four Vanwalls before practice.

Fangio with two motorcycle carabinieri.

Moss with the journalist Denis Jenkinson.

Road racing: the Centro Sud
Maseratis of Gregory and Bonnier.

Brooks.

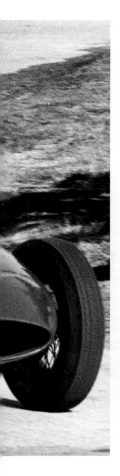

Clockwise from top left: Scarlatti, Behra, Schell and Godia.

Right: Musso in practice.

Below: Lewis-Evans.

The Coopers of Brabham (24) and Salvadori (22).

don't know. I wasn't terribly interested. I was too pre-occupied, believe you me. I don't remember anything about that race except feeling absolutely diabolical and trying to do what I thought was my duty to finish the race. I think I took the record for the maximum number of cups of tea drunk afterwards, though. In those days Sid Henshall was the Ferodo representative, and he went to all the races with his little caravan and canopy and he used to dispense tea after the event. I think I drank 17 cups of tea within the space of an hour and a half after that race. Not the best way to replace one's liquids, but that's what I did.'

A fortnight later, his wounds more or less healed, Brooks prepared to leave for Pescara. He was still living in Manchester, but he had recently swapped the transportation of his student days – an Austin A30, followed by a Ford Anglia – for a proper grand prix driver's conveyance: an Aston Martin DB2/4, bought from the factory. 'It was a very nice car, silver on the upper half of the body, black on the lower,' he said. But Brooks's characteristic prudence also came into play. 'They sold it to me for a half-decent price – it wasn't new. I think it must have been a demonstrator.'

For the drive down to the Adriatic, however, he opted for a humbler vehicle. His friend Roy Salvadori, a member of the Cooper works team, had a sideline writing road tests for a monthly magazine, and sometimes used the cars he was given as transportation to and from races. Salvadori would be driving down to Pescara in a Hillman Minx. Tony Brooks and Pina Resegotti, saving up to get married, went along for the ride.

6

Red

With ten cars on the grid, Maserati was not just the dominant make in sheer numbers and the most successful in terms of the current championship standings, but also the oldest by a long way. The Maserati brothers – Ernesto, Bindo, Alfieri and Ettore – built their first car in 1926 in their home city of Bologna, and entered it in the Targa Florio. Alfieri took the wheel with a friend, Guerino Bertocchi, as his riding mechanic; after covering the 336 miles of wild Sicilian mountain roads in eight and a half hours, they were placed ninth. Within a year they were entering a three-car team for a grand prix, and at the end of 1927 one of their cars came second in the Coppa Acerbo, behind Campari's Alfa P2. A year later Ernesto, also a talented driver, won the Coppa Acerbo Junior. Alfieri, the most dynamic of the brothers, died in 1932 as a result of a racing injury, but throughout the 1930s Maserati rivalled Alfa Romeo for the title of Italy's top racing team. Both would eventually fall away before the might of the Germans in international grand prix racing.

For all their gifts, the Maseratis were not great businessmen. They diversified their affairs, notably into the manufacture of spark plugs, and developed a small electric truck. In 1938, however, they were receptive to an approach from Count Adolfo Orsi, a Modena-based industrialist. Under the deal with Orsi the business was transferred to Modena, where the count's son, Omer, took over as managing director. The three surviving brothers agreed to stay on as consultants for a ten-year period, which turned out to encompass the war years. But now the Orsis were in control.

After the war the company resumed operations, building updated versions of their pre-war models for private customers and developing a new small sports car. The first race of 1946, the Nice Grand Prix, held over 65 laps of a 1.9-mile circuit through the streets of the town, was won by Luigi Villoresi in a Maserati. Their successes continued, and in 1948 their supercharged 4CLT model was driven to victory at San Remo by the young Alberto Ascari. The following winter the Argentine Automobile Club bought a similar car for Juan Manuel Fangio to campaign against the visiting Europeans in the annual Temporada series. Fangio used it well, impressing the visiting European teams by winning the Mar del Plata Grand Prix and finishing second in the Doña Eva Duarte Perón Grand Prix, held over the Palermo Park circuit in Buenos Aires. A few weeks later he also won at San Remo, and again at Pau, Perpignan and Albi, during his first full season of competition in Europe.

The next year Fangio joined the revived Alfa Romeo grand prix team, whose supremacy destroyed the immediate ambitions of Maserati and their Modenese neighbours, the fledgling Ferrari team. Fangio stayed with Alfa Romeo for 1951 and won his first world championship at the age of 41. But the team withdrew at the end of the season, leaving the Argentine to sign a two-year contract with Maserati. The 1952 season was terminated for him when, having driven overnight to Monza from a race in Ireland, he suffered the only serious crash of his career. Ascari cruised to the title that season in a Ferrari, and repeated his domination the following year, despite Fangio's return. Maserati had simply not kept up with technical developments.

They made a leap forward in 1954, however, when the arrival of a young engineer, Giulio Alfieri, enabled them to create a new machine. The 250F, as it was called, was designed to compete under the new Formula One regulations, which restricted cars to unsupercharged engines of no more than 2.5 litres (or supercharged ones of 750cc, which was not a serious option). The 250F turned out to be the most loved of all the grand prix cars of its era, not least by its drivers. Its engine, designed by Vittorio Bellentani and Alberto Massimino, might not have been the most powerful, but the rest of the package resulted in a fast, flexible and forgiving machine which suited most types of circuit and encouraged expressive driving, particularly the use of the four-wheel drift. It was also a thing of great beauty, to most eyes the ideal statement of the post-war single-seater front-engined racing car.

Fangio had signed a contract to drive for Mercedes-Benz in 1954 and 1955, but when the German cars were unready for the start of the 1954 season, he was allowed to make a temporary return to Maserati. Forming an immediate bond with the 250F, he won the first two races of the season, in Argentina and Belgium. But when Mercedes arrived at Rheims for the third round of the championship with their new streamlined machines, the party was over for the Italian teams. Until Mercedes departed at the end of 1955, their exit hastened by the dreadful crash at Le Mans in which 80 spectators and their own driver, Pierre Levegh, were killed, there were only thin pickings for Maserati and Ferrari. And even under the Orsis' regime, Maserati had made no significant provision for a period of sustained failure on the track.

For 1956 they signed up Stirling Moss as their number one driver. Moss had prospered during 1954 at the wheel of his own 250F, impressing the works team enough to earn an invitation to join them on a semi-official basis halfway through the season. In 1955 he left to join Fangio at Mercedes, but he was back a year later, with Jean Behra (a tough little Frenchman who had made an impression with the under-resourced Gordini team) as his number two. Moss profited from spending a season following in Fangio's wheeltracks, and in 1956 he showed himself to be very nearly the older man's equal, finishing the season only three points behind the maestro.

Moss's decision to join the Vanwall team for 1957 enabled Fangio to return to Maserati. After enduring a year of Ferrari's internal politics, the world champion was delighted to be back. 'Fangio always said that although Mercedes-Benz paid him well and looked after him, Maserati was his favourite team,' Bernard Cahier remembered. 'That was where his heart was.' He and Behra were joined by Harry Schell, a congenial Franco-American, with Giorgio Scarlatti, a solid Roman sports car driver, as the fourth team member. Behra and Schell were 36 years old; Scarlatti was a few months younger. Together with Fangio they formed an experienced team under the wise, sophisticated and tolerant management of Nello Ugolini, who had been the Scuderia Ferrari's first *direttore sportivo* back in the

1930s. Giulo Alfieri was looking after the development of the 250F, with a crew of mechanics supervised by Guerino Bertocchi, the company's most dedicated servant.

At 46, Fangio was in the final full season of his career. Within a year he would get out of his Maserati after finishing fourth at Rheims and say, 'No more.' He was the maestro, the unquestioned *patron* of the group, the only one to whom Moss deferred without question. His talent, his experience and his courteous manner put him above reproach. And occasionally, as he had at the Nürburgring, he could do something that would make them all shake their heads in wonder and admiration. 'He was the most natural driver around at the time,' Brooks said. 'He was so good that he could produce outstanding performances without exceeding his personal safety margins. Some of his qualities were anticipation, judgement, sensitivity in his hands and the seat of his pants, and of course great mental strength. He read a race very carefully and drove very intel-ligently. He was always one step ahead. But when you try to analyse exactly what gave him his edge, you come up against a stone wall.' Nor were his gifts confined to driving technique and racecraft. 'He was recognised not only as the best driver but as the fairest. I never heard a single complaint about his behaviour, in or out of the cockpit, and there aren't many world champions you could say that about. When he entered a room, it went quiet. His whole bearing was almost like royalty, but it was accompanied by considerable modesty. He commanded awe.'

Fangio's team-mates were contrasting types. The fast and brave Behra, born 36 years earlier in Nice, had started his career racing motorbikes, on which he became cham-pion of France three years running, before making his name with the beautiful little Gordini cars. In non-championship races he had been driving for BRM with some success, winning the Caen GP on the weekend between Aintree and the Nürburgring. 'Tough man, Behra – very successful, very good driver, very hairy,' Roy Salvadori remembered. 'Behra tended to keep to himself,' Brooks added, 'and he really only spoke French, so communicating with him wasn't easy, even though we were in the Ferrari team together in 1959.' To Moss, who had raced alongside Behra at Maserati the previous year, one professional characteristic marked him out: 'He was one of the few people who, if you passed him, you couldn't think, "Well, now I'll just get going." He'd hang on and have a go back. Not many would.'

Where Behra had enormous competitive intensity, and was beginning to fret about his failure to win a world championship grand prix, Harry Schell was celebrated for a much more happy-go-lucky attitude to life. Born in Paris in 1921, he was the son of a French father and an American mother, Laury Schell and Lucy O'Reilly Schell, who ran the Ecurie Bleue racing team. After his father died in a car crash, his mother took the team to Indianapolis, where she entered the great René Dreyfus in a Maserati. Harry went along, and after serving with the US Army in Finland during the Second World War he drove for the teams of Enrico Platé and Amedée Gordini, followed by spells with Maserati, Ferrari and Vanwall. Although he was a professional driver, Schell shared with Collins and Hawthorn some of the attitudes of an earlier era. 'Harry was a mate of everybody, really, very easy-going sort of guy, easy to get along with,' Moss said. Salvadori was unusually effusive: 'Harry Schell was a wonderful guy, a pound a minute. He'd liven life up. And he was getting better and better. He used to make some marvellous races, but you could never rely on it. Then you'd write him off and suddenly he'd give a performance. He drove a Vanwall at Rheims once and he was quicker than Hawthorn, much quicker. Now that's unbelievable. He got himself wound up and on this particular occasion he was incredibly quick.' But it was his *joie de vivre* that people remembered, and his capacity for playing practical jokes. 'I shouldn't think there's anybody like him today,' Brooks remarked.

Unlike Ferrari, the Maserati company was happy to sell grand prix cars to customers. The 250F was particularly popular with private entrants and amateur drivers, since it was robust, straightforward, a pleasant car to drive as well as a fast one, with no vices or secrets. Any reasonably competent driver could handle it in an approximation of the style of Moss or Fangio, employing the power to break the adhesion of the rear wheels while tweaking the steering on to opposite lock and getting the car balanced in a nice four-wheel drift.

At Pescara, as well as the four six-cylinder factory 250Fs and one with an experimental V12 engine, there were six private Maseratis. Two came from the Scuderia Centro Sud, an Italian team organised by Guglielmo Dei, Maserati's agent for southern Italy. It had started operations the previous year, entering 250Fs for a selection of drivers including the veterans Luigi Villoresi and Louis Chiron, but for 1957 the team had the status of a works-assisted effort. Painted white, the cars were to be driven by Masten Gregory, a young American, and Jo Bonnier, a bearded Swede. Gregory's car wore broad blue stripes down the centre and the flanks of the bodywork, white and blue being the racing colours of the United States; the other car had a double stripe of blue and gold, the colours of Sweden. The Centro Sud pair represented an odd mixture, sharing only a background of family wealth. Bonnier had begun his career by racing an Alfa Romeo on ice. By 1957 he had started to get drives with the Maserati sports car team, and had made his first appearance in one of Dei's 250Fs in Argentina, where he finished seventh. His talent was not particularly striking, although it was sufficient, less than three years after his grand prix debut, to make him the first man to win a world championship race at the wheel of a BRM. He also became a leading light in the Grand Prix Drivers' Association – a shop steward, it might be said, in the drivers' union.

The faster of the two Centro Sud men was a bespectacled 25-year-old from Kansas City. Masten Gregory was one of a group of drivers who arrived in Europe in the middle 1950s, a varied bunch who shared not only abundant funding but the quality – in European eyes – of seeming somehow larger than life. Like his compatriots, Gregory had raced European sports cars at home – in his case an Allard and a C-type Jaguar – before deciding to try his luck on the other side of the ocean. He arrived in Italy for the first time in 1954 with a Ferrari bought from the proceeds of an inheritance; three years later he was beginning to show considerable speed, if a lack of consistency. A chain-smoker, and as distinctive a character as the others, he had a look that would be associated, 20 years later, with the young Woody Allen.

To the other drivers, he was a bit of an enigma. 'A mystery man,' Salvadori said. 'He could put a spurt on during a race and go like stink, and you'd be thinking, "This guy is really going to do things," and suddenly he'd fade. I don't want to go any further than that, but it was so unnatural.' To

Moss, who raced with him in sports cars, 'He was an incredible character. 'He was the only guy I've known who, if he saw a shunt coming, he'd get out of the car and watch it. But he was quite quick. He just hadn't got the stamina.'

The remaining four 250Fs were entered by their owners. Luigi Piotti, a 43-year-old businessman and part-time racer, brought his own car. So did Francesco Godia Sales of Barcelona, another gentleman racer, who had made his grand prix debut in 1951 and had been given the wheel of a factory car in 1956. Bruce Halford, a 26-year-old from Hampton-in-Arden, near Birmingham, and Horace Gould, a 35-year-old garage proprietor from Bristol in his third season on the Continent, were well-known faces on the English club racing scene who had bought their own Maseratis and were enjoying a season doing the rounds of the Formula One races, living from race to race on starting money. This was a way of life made possible by the existence of numerous non-championship races at such places as Syracuse, Pau, Caen and Naples, where the organisers were prepared to spend a little money in order to attract a decent entry of current machinery, knowing that most of the factory teams and their star drivers would not be attending. The 250F was the mainstay of these secondary races; without Maserati's desire to improve their own financial position by selling their cars, the fields would have been much thinner. And their readiness to repair and rebuild their customers' cars created good relationships.

'There was a very relaxed atmosphere in that team,' Cahier said. 'Nice people, no tension from politics. Really a friendly place. You could go to the factory any time and Giulio Alfieri would show you everything. Omer Orsi was a nice person, too. And Fangio adored Bertocchi. The Ferrari team was much more stiff; not the same atmosphere at all.'

The first car bearing the Ferrari name had not appeared until the spring of 1947, but by the time the team's transporter turned up at Pescara, 10 years later, the Scuderia had already known extremes of triumph and humiliation. The successes of 1952 and 1953, when Ascari won nine grands prix in a row, had been extraordinary. Combined with the early victories in the Mille Miglia, the 24 Hours of Le Mans and the Targa Florio, and with the curiously magnetic quality of Enzo Ferrari's opaque personality, they laid the foundations of a myth which would bring playboys, movie stars and royalty flocking to the doors of the Maranello factory, anxious to buy a sports or grand touring car that would invest them, too, with some of the dark glamour associated with the name.

Unlike the people who had founded Maserati and those who were now running it, Enzo Ferrari had an intuitive understanding of what it would take to keep his company running. He had always been a hustler and a fixer. Before the war he had assembled the backing from rich amateur drivers and commercial companies that enabled him to run the Scuderia at a comfortable profit. Now he knew, long before marketing became a science, how to build an image that would carry the company through the sort of lean period that began, quite unexpectedly, in 1954, when the arrival of Mercedes exposed the inadequacy of his latest racing cars. The defection of Ascari and his number two, Villoresi, to the new Lancia team darkened Enzo Ferrari's mood. His own new model, a bulbous four-cylinder machine known as the Squalo for its supposed resemblance to a shark, performed in a way that matched its unpleasant looks, the team's only successes coming when Ferrari responded to the pleas of his drivers and produced an updated version of the previous year's car. Even then they had to rely on misfortune striking down the Germans.

In competitive terms, Ferrari was on the rocks by the middle of 1955. So profound was the decline that he had even been threatening to pull out of racing, the first of several such Olympian sulks. Salvation arrived, however, when Lancia, which had spent two years developing a new and technologically adventurous V8-engined grand prix car, decided to give up, crippled by the cost and by the death of Ascari, their number-one driver, in a testing accident. Under a curious deal, the company, including the racing team, had fallen into the hands of a cement manufacturer with no interest in the sport. Enzo Ferrari talked to Gianni Agnelli, the young son of the founder of Fiat and already one of his customers. Agnelli in turn talked to the cement manufacturer, and agreed a deal whereby Fiat would pay for the entire racing team to be transferred to Ferrari's ownership. And so one day in the autumn of 1955 Ferrari received six sparkling Lancia D50 racing cars, plus their drivers, Eugenio Castellotti and Mike Hawthorn, their designer, Vittorio Jano, and their technical director, Luigi Bazzi, an old friend of Enzo Ferrari from the pre-war Scuderia. Suddenly Ferrari had got himself a brand-new team.

By the start of the 1956 season he had also acquired a brand-new driver, for Juan Manuel Fangio no longer had a Mercedes to drive and could see that the combination of Lancia's advanced technology and the professional experience of the Scuderia Ferrari would take some beating.

Fangio and Ferrari disliked and distrusted each other on sight, but the combination was effective enough to win the title, Fangio's fourth. The D50 was heavily modified, most obviously by moving its petrol tanks from panniers between the wheels to a more conventional location in the tail (while leaving the distinctive panniers in place); it was good enough to allow Fangio to win three of that season's seven races, finishing ahead of Moss, his former Mercedes team-mate but now Maserati's team leader, in the championship standings. At the end of the season Fangio and Ferrari parted company with a sense of relief and a few harsh words in both directions.

Without the world champion, whose personal reputation overshadowed that of his machinery, Enzo Ferrari was able to assemble a collection of the sort of drivers he particularly liked: young men still establishing their reputations, full of ambition, who would race among themselves to the greater glory of his cars. For his front-line cars in 1957 he had two Italians, Eugenio Castellotti of Milan and Luigi Musso of Rome; two British drivers, Mike Hawthorn of Surrey and Peter Collins of the West Midlands; and a Spanish noble-man, Alfonso de Portago, otherwise Don Alfonso Antonio Cabeza de Vaca y Leighton, Carvajal and Ayre, the seven-teenth Marquès de Portago and the twelfth Count of Mejorada. Castellotti and Collins were 26, Hawthorn was 27, Portago was 28 and Musso was 33. A new version of Lancia-Ferrari, now known simply as the Ferrari 801, retained the V8 engine that Jano had designed for Lancia but featured a different front suspension and a modified frame which carried smoother bodywork, minus the distinctive pan-niers. With four long megaphone exhausts exposed along the bottom of each of the car's broad flanks, it was a handsome machine which, in contrast to the more feline Maserati 250F, appeared to exude brute power.

But in Buenos Aires, as the drivers chased round after Fangio, it became obvious that although the 801 might have a rugged chassis and more horsepower at its disposal, it lacked the thoroughbred qualities of the 250F. All six Ferraris retired; the team manager, Eraldo Sculati, was sacked on his return and replaced by Mino Amorotti. At Monaco, the Vanwall team added itself to Ferrari's list of problems. Moss led the race from pole position until precipitating the accident that removed Hawthorn and Collins. They were eclipsed again at Aintree, where first Moss's Vanwall and then Behra's 250F dominated the grand prix. A win in the German Grand Prix looked likely when Fangio made a pit stop for fuel and tyres and not only forfeited a substantial lead but returned to the race 50 seconds in arrears of Hawthorn and Collins. His successful chase of Ferrari's two young Englishmen immediately jumped to the top of motor racing's list of legendary feats.

In the four-month gap between the races in Argentina and Monaco, however, two terrible events had blighted the Scuderia's season. First, Castellotti was killed at the Modena autodrome while testing the 801. He had been telephoned in Florence, where he was staying with his fiancée, the actress Delia Scala, and told that his presence was required early the next morning because Behra was breaking local records with the new Maserati and a response was required. Castellotti rose at dawn and drove through the Apennines to save the honour of Ferrari, but by evening he was dead. Second, a blown tyre at 175mph had thrown De Portago's 3.5-litre Ferrari sports car off the road near the end of the Mille Miglia, killing nine spectators, five of them children, along with the Spaniard and his co-driver. Immediately Enzo Ferrari was deemed a slaughterer of innocents; politicians joined the Vatican in calling for an end to all motor racing, and some even suggested that the man who built the car should be prosecuted.

In Italy the furore lasted all summer, and by the time Pescara was inserted into the calendar, Enzo Ferrari felt he had endured enough. No one, he said, had come to his aid while he was being so gratuitously attacked from all quarters. There were also rumours that one more fatal accident involving a Ferrari would lead to criminal charges. Even though the race was in Italy, he said, he would not be sending his cars. In fact he would not be racing in Italy ever again. Indeed, he might even disband his team altogether.

As the decades went by, it became apparent that although Ferrari's own workers never took industrial action, a protest strike was the old man's favourite way of making his point, even when he seemed to be cutting off his own very handsome nose to spite his face. Sometimes he found a solution that enabled him to compete without losing face. But this time, he told his drivers, he was adamant that the Gran Premio di Pescara would take place without Ferrari's participation.

Luigi Musso was distraught. Without actually managing to win a race, all season long he had been quietly amassing places and points – second in the French Grand Prix, second at Aintree, fourth at the Nürburgring. Now, with only two races left, he had 16 points to Fangio's 34, with Hawthorn on 13, Brooks on 10, and Moss and Collins on 8. With 8 points awarded for a win and an extra point for the fastest lap in the race, Musso could not overtake Fangio, but he could certainly defend his second place, worth a great deal in prestige. Now he was being denied even that opportunity, by his own employer.

The son of a Roman diplomat, Musso had grown up in a *palazzo* off the Via Veneto, where his father kept a remarkable collection of Chinese art. He had worked his way up through sports car racing at the wheel of a little Maserati, and his girlfriends included Maria Teresa De Filippis, a gamine girl from a good family and one of the few women even to attempt to break into grand prix racing. She was followed in his affections by Fiamma Breschi, a beautiful blonde teenager who accompanied him to the races during his last two years on earth. It was for *la bionda* that Musso left his wife and two children. In the cockpit, he sometimes wore a polo shirt trimmed with the maroon and yellow colours of AS Roma, his favourite football team. His helmet was yellow, with a small Italian *tricolore* painted on each side.

Like several Italians of his generation, Musso felt the pressure to provide his country with another world champion. 'Now I am alone,' he had written in the newspaper *Paese Sera* after Castellotti's fatal accident, listing also the deaths of Varzi, Nuvolari, Bonetto and Ascari, and the retirements of Villoresi and Farina. At Rheims in July, in the non-championship Grand Prix of the Marne, he beat the Maseratis of Fangio and Behra, the Vanwalls of Lewis-Evans and Salvadori and his team-mate Hawthorn to record his first major victory since Pescara in 1954, receiving a prize of 10 million francs. He had come of age, the Italian sports papers said; now he would show the world that he was a world champion in the making.

To Moss, Musso was 'a clean driver, quite fast, very comparable with Peter Collins and Castellotti. Musso,

Collins, Castellotti and Hawthorn were all comparable. Hawthorn on his day would probably be a little bit better, but overall not.' Brooks had first met the Italian at Syracuse in 1955, when Musso was driving a private 250F, and had raced against him many times. 'I spoke Italian by then,' Brooks said, 'but I never got to know him well. I don't remember saying more than hello and goodbye to him. He always struck me as being slightly aloof, but that's purely from a distance.' To Salvadori, 'Musso was OK, very nationalistic like all Italians. Pleasant enough guy. They all were, although there were tough nuts, like Farina, that you didn't want to get near, real toughies.'

Now, through no fault of his own, Musso was being denied the chance to fight for Italy's honour. He needed to look elsewhere, and Enzo Ferrari agreed to release him just for the one race. An approach to Maserati, Ferrari's bitterest rivals, was made. Musso had, after all, begun his career in their cars. But, as the correspondent of *Motor Racing* magazine reported, 'they did not seem very interested in having one of the Ferrari team take a possible second place in the world championship from their own drivers.' The only other competitive car was the Vanwall. Musso called Tony Vandervell, to be courteously informed that three cars had been entered for the race and all three had their nominated drivers. They would be taking a fourth car, but it would be needed as a spare.

The Automobile Club di Pescara, worried that the reduced entry would diminish the appeal of their great opportunity to put on a championship round, explored various avenues in order to get Hawthorn and Collins into the race, as well as Musso. They had no luck. Bankruptcy was about to overwhelm Connaught, and the same went for Gordini;

neither was in a position to finance a team for one race. The organisers contacted BRM, whose activities had ground to a halt again after the team temporarily ran out of drivers: Mackay-Fraser had been killed at Rheims, Flockhart was recovering from his crash at Rouen, and Behra and Schell, who drove occasionally for the team in non-championship races, were contracted to Maserati. At Aintree they had entered Les Leston and Jack Fairman, two English journeymen, and the general view of the BRM operation was voiced when Moss ran into Leston in the paddock and remarked, 'Oh, so you saw the small ad in *Exchange and Mart*, did you?' Having decided to withdraw from the last three rounds of the championship, they were unable to respond to the last-minute request.

As a final resort, Musso went back and pleaded with Ferrari. Eventually the old man relented. He would send one of the 801s, with a skeleton crew of mechanics, as a sort of semi-private entry. It would be a token effort, intended solely to salve Musso's pride. Hawthorn and Collins were left to kick their heels.

7
Green

The Vanwalls arrived in Pescara a month after their famous victory at Aintree, where Stirling Moss and Tony Brooks had shared victory in the British Grand Prix: the first ever win in a championship *grande épreuve* for a British car driven by a British driver (or, in this case, drivers). Since that historic afternoon they had been badly defeated at the Nürburgring, where their suspension had proved unequal to the challenge of 174 corners in 14 miles. But the problem was quickly ironed out, like most of the problems Tony Vandervell (the 'Van' in Vanwall) found himself facing.

Vandervell was the sort of figure known to British newspaper readers of the 1950s as a 'millionaire industrialist'. A million was then an unimaginably large amount of money, and Britain still possessed a manufacturing industry of significant dimensions. If you wanted bicycles, you went to Nottingham; if you wanted motorbikes, you went to Birmingham; if you wanted cars, you went to Oxford or Coventry; if you wanted bearings, you went to Tony Vandervell's factory in Acton, West London. But making bearings did not satisfy Vandervell's soul. It was merely the platform from which he would attempt to achieve his true ambition.

Born in 1898, six months after Enzo Ferrari, he also fitted the subtler details of the archetypal millionaire industrialist, being simultaneously a maverick risk-taker and a suffer-no-fools conservative. Both characteristics fitted him for the task that took over his life: to build a British racing car that would beat the best the Continent had to offer.

'He was a sort of English version of Ferrari, or trying to be,' Stirling Moss said. 'He didn't like Ferrari, he didn't like what he called "the bloody red cars", and so on, but there's no doubt that he was very Ferrari-ish in his temperament. I suppose he was influenced by Ferrari, but he'd never admit it. Tony achieved amazing things with his car, but never what Ferrari had done. Let's face it, that was something quite different. He was gruff, certainly. I didn't mind him, I must say, because he was actually quite an enthusiast. And I think he was patriotic. Patriotism doesn't exist now, there's no such thing, but in those days it was quite important and I think the fact that he could make a green car that would beat the Italians gave him a tremendous kick.'

Educated at Harrow, Vandervell was academically restless but loved sport. His father, an electrical engineer, had begun a small business called C. A. Vandervell and Co. in Willesden Green in 1892, and tended its growth. In 1913, the year Tony joined the company, CAV's workers fitted the lighting to Queen Mary's new Daimler, and the business had expanded into the manufacture of tools and precision instruments. After service as an engineer in the First World War, Tony began to spend his spare time competing in speed trials, hill climbs and circuit races. When CAV was sold to Joseph Lucas Ltd, he was put in charge of another company, bought by his father in the hope that it would deflect his interest away from fast cars and West End nightlife. Within a year he had secured from a US firm a licence to manufacture in Europe a revolutionary new type of 'Thin Wall' bearing, having sat and slept for six days in the outer office of a director of the Cleveland company before finally receiving the consent he required. His persistence was amply rewarded. At a new factory on Western Avenue in Acton, Vandervell Products Ltd began to churn out the bearings. By the middle of the 1930s they had become standard equipment on all cars, and Vandervell's fortune was made.

Soon after the end of the Second World War, in which he had assisted on the development of aero engines, Vandervell was approached by Raymond Mays, an English racing driver of the pre-war era who was now involved, with his partner, Peter Berthon, in setting up a project to build a British grand prix car. Keen on the idea, Vandervell joined the board of British Racing Motors and put his company at the disposal of the design team as they worked on their remarkably complex 1500cc V16 engine, with its tiny cylinders and a supercharger developed by Rolls-Royce from those used on the Merlin engines of Spitfires, Hurricanes and Lancasters.

The BRM suffered from the late delivery of parts during the industrial confusion of the post-war era, but it suffered more from the over-ambition of its designers and the sclerotic nature of the project's decision-making processes. Long before it became apparent to the outside world that the BRM was a fiasco in the making, Vandervell had forcefully expressed his reservations. Since the BRM team had a Ministry of Supply permit to acquire a single racing car from abroad for the purposes of research and comparison, and since Vandervell Products Ltd were already supplying engine bearings for the Scuderia Ferrari's cars, he suggested that the team should try to purchase one of Enzo Ferrari's current grand prix cars, for use as a sort of test bed for their own programme. But by the time the car arrived, after complicated negotiations and much delay (and at a cost of £4360 plus £5430 in duty and purchase tax), it was obvious that they had been sent an obsolete model, leading to brusque exchanges between Vandervell and Ferrari. The two companies continued to collaborate, but when a second car was delivered it proved little better than the first. It was raced, however, in green paint and under the name 'Thinwall Special'. This was an idea Vandervell may have picked up during a wartime visit to the Indianapolis 500 race, where the cars were named after their sponsors; it would take another couple of decades for the practice to catch on in Europe.

As the original BRM project ran itself into the ground in a series of embarrassing failures on the track, so Vandervell began to pay more attention to his own little racing team. The Ferrari was a good basis for working out his ideas of what he thought a grand prix car should be, and by 1952 he was exploring the possibility of building his own car, using various advanced concepts. He went to Girling and Goodyear to talk about disc brakes, he went to John Cooper's Surbiton garage to talk about chassis design, he talked to Bosch in Germany about fuel injection, and he had his own engineers working on the idea of putting four 500cc Norton motorcycle engines together to make a two-litre powerplant conforming to the Formula Two regulations under which grands prix were run in 1952–3. Meanwhile he was still sending the now heavily modified Ferrari out to compete in the hands of a variety of drivers, to get some experience of running a racing team. His new car, the first to race under the name Vanwall, made its debut in 1954 in the hands of Alan Brown, and was later driven by Peter Collins, Mike Hawthorn, Harry Schell and Ken Wharton, without much success. But motor racing had already moved on, and even BRM – now owned by another millionaire industrialist, Sir Alfred Owen – had already built a new car for the 2.5-litre formula. Vandervell instructed his engineers to do the same in time for the 1956 season.

The four-cylinder Norton-based engine was expanded in capacity, but several other major elements of the car were to break new ground. Colin Chapman, whose lightweight Lotus sports cars were setting a trend, was invited in to redesign the chassis frame, and he brought along Frank Costin, a former aerodynamic flight test engineer in the experimental department of the De Havilland aircraft company. Costin designed a wind-cheating body that could have come from a jet fighter, a smoothly contoured design with a narrow opening for the radiator in the nose, a high, rounded tail, a wrap-around cockpit and a flush-fitting exhaust pipe. For the first time, real aerodynamic theory, as opposed to comic-book guesswork, was being brought to bear on a racing car. His task had not been easy: the four-cylinder engine was tall, carrying exposed valve gear, and the driver sat high above the driveshaft, making it difficult for the designer to reduce the car's frontal area. But Costin found an elegant solution and the result, as the motoring critic L. J. K. Setright wrote, was 'an oddly broad and bulbous shape which was nevertheless superbly smooth and curvilinear'. When the new car appeared at Silverstone on 5 May 1956 for the *Daily Express* International Trophy Race, it caused a sensation – not just through its looks, but by its performance. Two cars were entered, and they came first and second, ahead of the full Ferrari team, led by Juan Manuel Fangio. In the second Vanwall was Harry Schell. And in the first, having started from pole position and broken the absolute lap record for the course while averaging more than 100mph for the entire race, was Stirling Moss, generously loaned by Maserati for a race to which they had not sent an entry.

Two months later, with Moss back in a red car, Schell and Hawthorn appeared in the Vanwalls for the French Grand Prix at Rheims, where the car's promise was confirmed. Since his own car was giving spasmodic trouble, and since Hawthorn had just finished competing in the 24-hour sports car race, the two of them swapped mounts soon after the start. Schell used the Vanwall's impressive speed on the long straights to make up the time and overhaul the leading group of three Lancia-Ferraris, whose drivers found it hard to believe that he was on the same lap as them. When they realised the truth, Fangio, Collins and Castellotti upset Vandervell by working together to give Schell a hard time, baulking and blocking him as he got among them. For British fans the sight of a green car dicing on equal terms with the Italians was like something from a dream, but they were forced to wake up when the Vanwall eventually fell back, suffering from fuel-injection problems. Schell confirmed the good impression at Monza, in the last race of the year, when he fought Moss for the lead in the early stages before succumbing to transmission trouble.

....

By this time Moss had become convinced that the Vanwall was the car to drive in 1957. He was 27 years old, and time was pressing. His ambition had always been not merely to win the world championship but to win it in a British car, and it had led him up some blind alleys earlier in his career. The decision to join Mercedes and Maserati had not been taken lightly. Now his chance had come. Initially he had been unsure about the Vanwall's reliability, having watched Schell break down on numerous occasions. But test drives at Oulton Park, Silverstone and Goodwood, during which he covered a full 300-mile grand prix distance on each occasion, helped him make up his mind, even though none of the tests was completed without some niggling problem or other. And on 31 October 1956 the announcement was made. The terms of his contract, which were not made public, were a retainer of £5000, to be paid in equal instalments after each *grande épreuve*, plus starting money of £500 for each round of the world championship and £400 for other races, plus 60 per cent of all bonuses. Out of this he was to pay his travel and hotel expenses.

Now that Moss was in place, Vandervell only needed a second driver for what was initially intended to be a two-car team. Schell, despite his willing performances of the previous year, had been dropped, cruelly but accurately judged to be not quite good enough to win grands prix. Having admired the performances of Tony Brooks, Vandervell and David Yorke issued an invitation to another test session at Oulton Park. Again the results were satisfactory and a deal was concluded in November, but negotiations to reach an agreement with Aston Martin, to whom Brooks was contracted to drive in sports car races, delayed an appointment until February 1957.

Over the winter the cars were rebuilt to incorporate various modifications, including the Chapman-inspired addition of coil springs in the rear suspension. Moss, as was his wont, made several suggestions. Like the other drivers, he complained that the car's acceleration was hampered by a flat spot low down the rev range. Vandervell was reluctant to accept the criticism, but Moss eventually succeeded in getting the message through to the engineering staff, and also proposed other small changes as a result of his test drives.

During the season Moss communicated his requirements through David Yorke, a tall, elegant figure, or directly to Cyril Atkins, the chief mechanic. And sometimes he would go directly to the top. 'David Yorke had the title of team manager, but that's not really what he was,' Moss said. 'In those days the drivers would manage themselves, according to the information given from the pits. Very few team managers would ever make you go faster, in case you hurt yourself. If you put out a sign that says, "Go faster" and the guy goes and hurts himself, that's a tremendous responsibility. I think they liked to give you information so that you could say to yourself, "God, I'd better go quicker, or so-and-so's going to catch me up." They'd quite often put out a sign saying "EZ" or come out and slow you down. John Wyer at Aston Martin was a tactician. I wouldn't say David was. Vandervell would decide where we were going to race, and David would then take over and see that it happened. Vandervell would make the decisions but other people had to carry them out for him. And in those days everybody mucked in much more. You didn't have the structure they have now. It was a group, really.'

Halfway through the 1957 season the group was

expanded through the addition of a third car for Stuart Lewis-Evans, who had impressed the team when operating as an emergency stand-in at Rouen and Rheims. Aged 28, Lewis-Evans was married, with two children, and weighed no more than eight stone. Although heat was often a problem, drivers in those days did not need to develop powerful muscles. Lewis-Evans, however, was a feather-weight by any standards. A broad corset-like belt, often worn on top of his overalls, was another indication of his frailty. 'Stuart was quick,' Moss said, 'but unfortunately his biggest problem was a physical one. He wasn't a weakling, but when you've got someone as spindly as that, you wonder whether they've got the necessary stamina. It always struck me that he wasn't really that strong. But he drove very quickly. If I was learning a corner, it took me a long time to build up to the point I wanted to reach. He'd go straight to his limit and say, "Christ, that was a bit quick – I'd better go slower next time." '

Unknown to anyone, including himself, Lewis-Evans was suffering from a duodenal ulcer that would remain undiag-nosed until the end of the season. 'He wasn't what you'd call a super-fit guy,' his friend and mentor Bernie Eccles-tone said. 'He used to get a lot of colds, things like that. But sometimes he was so quick that he was an embar-rassment to Stirling and Tony. They'd take his engine and put it in their car, or take his car and put their engine in it, and it wouldn't worry him. He didn't care about them.'

All the drivers were struck by how little the atmosphere of the Vanwall team resembled that of any other grand prix outfit they had seen. Elsewhere, mechanics wore dirty overalls and allowed pools of oil to accumulate on the garage floor. That was the way things had always been done in businesses with their origins in backstreet garages. Within the Vanwall workshops inside the big white art deco factory on Western Avenue, however, engineers worked to a very contrasting set of standards, their meticulous behaviour imported from the experience of running a business manufacturing precision equipment for clients of substance. That was the way Tony Vandervell wanted it, and that was the way it would be.

The Cooper Car Company was a very different sort of undertaking. Whereas the Vanwalls were built on one of London's main industrial arteries, Cooper cars were designed and bolted together in a little two-storey garage at the bottom of a hill in leafy Surbiton, a name almost literally synonymous with suburban Surrey. At the front of the building was a forecourt with petrol pumps, and on the rough floor inside the garage John Cooper and his collaborators chalked the diagrams of the frames for the cars they were about to build: cars that were to change the world of motor racing.

The garage had been started by John Cooper's father, Charles, after the First World War. Charles Cooper had worked as a mechanic on S. F. Edge's mighty Napier, among the first cars to run at Brooklands; later he acted as manager to Kaye Don, another famous Brooklands driver. Charles and his wife Elsie drove AC cars, manufactured in nearby Thames Ditton, in long-distance trials, and for their son's eighth birthday they gave John his first car, a home-built motorcycle-engined special. At 12 he was upgraded to another special based round an Austin Seven engine and capable of 90mph. After wartime service on Admiralty secret projects, including miniature submarines, John joined his father's business and built his own little racing car in 1946, using suspension parts and steering gear from a couple of Fiat Topolinos, a Triumph motorcycle gearbox, and a 500cc engine from a JAP speedway bike. Designed for the new Formula Three, it went well enough to encourage Cooper to produce a dozen replicas for customers, including the 18-year-old Stirling Moss. Within a couple of years Cooper was fulfilling orders from around the world for his deceptively spidery machines, which could also take 1000cc engines and run in sprints and hill climbs. But it was in Formula Three that the cars made Cooper's reputation, in the hands of young drivers such as Moss, Peter Collins and Stuart Lewis-Evans.

When they entered Formula Two in 1952 it was with a comparatively conventional front-engined machine powered by a Bristol engine. Yet after one of the cars had helped Mike Hawthorn make his name when he chased the 4.5-litre Ferrari of the mighty González at Goodwood, the experiment with convention was set aside. Pitted against the Formula Two Ferraris and Maseratis, the Cooper-Bristol showed agility but lacked the power to offer a consistent challenge on the faster circuits. Cooper decided to go back to his original principles, and a 1100cc rear-engined sports car appeared in 1955. Its immediate success led directly to another Formula Two car, this time with its engine behind the driver. It was this car, which won its first race at Silverstone in 1956 in the hands of Roy Salvadori, that set the pattern for Cooper's future.

The car was unusually light, as the 500cc machines had been. It had a neat and practical layout, devised by Cooper and his new design partner, Owen Maddock. Pared of all excess, it was nevertheless sturdy enough to withstand the abuse it might receive from his customers, many of them amateur drivers who needed something robust for their weekend racing. And it was powered by a 1500cc engine built by Coventry Climax, a company which had specialised during the war in producing engines for mobile fire pumps. After the war Coventry Climax's design staff included Wally Hassan, an employee of Bentley during the glory years of success at Le Mans. He and his assistant, Harry Mundy, created a new lightweight 1100cc engine which was intended for use with fire pumps but was easily adapted for use as a full racing engine, with Kieft, Lotus and Cooper as their first customers. Bored out to a capacity of 1500cc, the engines produced power with reliability; just as important, the aluminium cylinder block enabled them to match the desire of the British chassis designers to produce a car weighing as little as possible, a significant factor given that these cars were raced mostly over the relatively smooth asphalt of disused airfields and had little need of the ruggedness with which their Italian and French counterparts were endowed.

It was Charles Cooper, then in his sixties, who yearned to see the cars bearing the family name competing in full grands prix against the very best opposition. To many it would have seemed a ludicrous aspiration. But at the beginning of 1957, encouraged by the performance of the Formula Two machines when entered in races with Formula One machinery, John Cooper explored the possibility of stretching the Climax engine to two litres. The project was sponsored by Rob Walker, a private entrant, and the result made its first appearance at Monte Carlo in May. The car was driven by Jack Brabham, a 31-year-old Australian who had turned up at the garage two years earlier with practical ideas about how to make his Cooper go faster and so impressed the management of the little company that he was eventually taken on as a works driver.

Brabham had learnt to handle racing cars on the dirt tracks of Australia, and his muscular approach to driving was far from that of the young gentlemen of the British racing scene. A formidable opponent, he was not to be trifled with. Even on the smooth asphalt of England's converted airfields, he tended to let the tail of his car hang out until it ran over the grass, scattering grass and stones in his wake. At Monte Carlo he seemed as out of place as an all-in wrestler at a vicarage tea party, but by the time his fuel pump mounting broke near the end of the Monaco Grand Prix he had shown that he could exploit the little car's nimbleness to the full, hurling it up into third place against the assembled Maseratis, Ferraris, Vanwalls and BRMs. As he pushed the broken car over the line to claim sixth place, the applause from the grandstands rang long and loud. And along the pits, other teams could not help but take notice of what had been going on, fuelled by sweat and ingenuity, in a humble little garage in Surbiton.

8

Salvadori

The sound of racing engines reached up and crashed off the walls of Roy Salvadori's apartment. Seven flights below, a couple of dozen Formula 3000 cars were practising for the race in support of the Monaco Grand Prix. Salvadori has lived in this block since the 1970s, with Sue Hindmarsh, the daughter of a man who won the 24 Hours of Le Mans in 1935 and died testing a Hawker Hurricane over St George's Hill, Weybridge three years later. Their apartment overlooks the start line on the Quai Albert 1er. More than half the circuit is visible from his balcony, including the climb from Sainte-Devote up to the Casino square and the dash from the chicane down the harbour side and through the left-hander that is still known as Tabac: two features essentially unchanged since Monaco's roads were first closed for a motor race in 1929. On race day the apartment is rented out to corporate hospitality people while the Salvadoris spend the day with friends whose quarters also provide a view of the race. Meanwhile their unknown guests get the chance to enjoy the ambience created by a few handsome trophies in display cases ('Not many, I'm afraid – most of them went to the team'), scale models of a handful

Behra in practice.

Moss in practice.

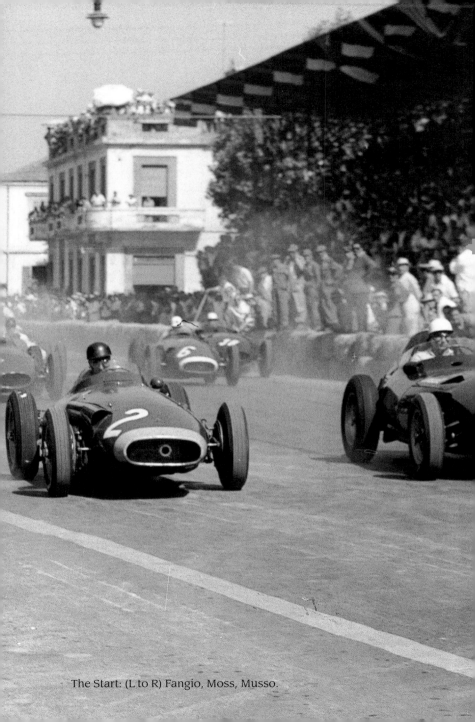

The Start: (L to R) Fangio, Moss, Musso.

Moss
during
the race.

Musso
during
the race.

Fangio
during the race.

A pit stop for Scarlatti.

Halford.

Moss comes in for a pit stop.

Moss during a pit stop.

The finish.

Moss with Tony Vandervell.

Moss with his father.

Moss with Fangio.

Moss with the victory bouquet, listening to the national anthem.

of the cars Salvadori drove, and some atmospheric paintings, including one of Sue's father driving his Lagonda at
Le Mans. The corporate guests are unlikely, however, to
recognise that this is the home of a man who finished
fourth in the world championship table in 1958.

In his open-necked shirt, well-pressed slacks and soft
suede loafers, Salvadori at 82 looked more than ever like a
well-preserved Hollywood star from the era of Gregory Peck
and Cary Grant. His companion, dressed like an off-duty
Audrey Hepburn in a crisp shirt and pedal-pushers, dis-
played a similar glamour, understated and timeless.

Salvadori's parents were born near Lucca, that beautiful
walled town in the Garfagnana, the hilly region of northern
Tuscany. Not so beautiful, perhaps, in the early years of the
20th century, when they left the family farm and emigrated
to Britain. It was a successful move. They settled in Dovercourt, near Harwich, where Salvadori's father opened an
ice-cream factory and was soon supplying much of the
south of England.

'They came to England together,' Salvadori said. 'I don't
know exactly when, but I was born in 1922 and they'd
arrived well before that. My father manufactured ice cream
and I think he had about 20 wagons delivering it during the
season. In those days making ice cream was quite an art. I
remember we weren't very popular. We were in a very good
district – Dovercourt is all retired majors and generals – so
you can imagine this Italian lot that's just arrived and
they're producing ice cream and working on a Sunday. I
didn't learn to speak Italian but I could understand when
my mother and father told me off in Italian. I know all of
the bad words.' In the winter he sometimes went to join
his mother in the resort of Viareggio, where his father

owned a pâtisserie, rented to the town's mayor, and a five-bedroomed flat on the front.

By the middle of the 1950s he had established himself as one of Britain's top racing drivers, a hard-nosed professional who thought nothing of competing in four or five different events during the course of a single day at Goodwood, Silverstone or Brands Hatch. He would race Formula One and Formula Two cars, sports cars, grand touring cars and saloon cars. 'Do you know the drill? We'd go to the British Grand Prix and at ten o'clock in the morning I'd be driving a sports car in the 1500cc class, at half past eleven I'd drive in the unlimited sports car race, both of them maybe 125-mile races, which was about an hour and a quarter, then you'd drive in the Formula One race, which was 300 miles, and you'd finish with a GT race. You'd be racing from ten in the morning until maybe half past five in the afternoon. If it was pissing with rain you'd be soaked, drenched, you'd have used up your spare pair of overalls on the second race and you'd be sitting in your damp overalls. But it used to happen very quickly, one race after the other. And that's what you had to do to make any sensible money. But, of course, there were four chances of doing well. And I always thought it helped in another way: we already knew the circuits well, but you'd know whether any oil had been spilt or where the road was loose. You were right up to date on it. And there weren't too many people who could do that, fortunately. Swapping from car to car is very difficult. I'd be driving a disc-braked car, then a drum-braked car, going from an engine that revved to seven-five to another that went to five-eight, one of them has a preselector gearbox and the other's got a five-speed box. The first lap, you don't know. You're thinking, is that corner flat? What car am I driving? But for some funny reason, I can't remember making too many mistakes.'

On 5 May 1951, however, he was read the last rites after crashing heavily at Silverstone's Stowe Corner in a Frazer-Nash sports car. 'It took me six months to recover,' he said, 'but I was racing again within about two or three.' Five years later to the day, at about the same time of the afternoon, at the same corner, while lying second in his private Maserati to Moss's Vanwall in the International Trophy, he left the track when his universal joint seized and the rear wheels locked. 'I was thrown out and knocked unconscious and I was taken to Northampton General, the worst hospital in England, and screwed back together. They discharged me with broken ribs, which turned up later.'

Although he was best known for his prowess in sports cars, and particularly for an enduring relationship with Aston Martin, he had campaigned the Maserati sufficiently well to be offered a drive in the BRM grand prix team for 1957, he and Ron Flockhart replacing the disenchanted Brooks and Hawthorn. 'It was meant to be a long-term arrangement,' he said, 'but I only drove the BRM twice, at Goodwood and Monaco. I knew they'd been in trouble with brakes. From memory, they had this single rear disc brake on the gearbox, and it was jamming on. As I understood it, they weren't going to modify the brakes themselves. Lockheed were going to do it. But we got to Goodwood, and coming up to the line it almost felt that the engine was seizing. The brakes were locking on and we couldn't move it. We had to hump it backwards and forwards, and eventually we did free it. But on the first lap the brake came on and never went off. It just locked up. So we didn't do a lap. Then we came to Monaco, and all I remember is going down through the Casino square and past the Tip-Top bar and the car just slowed and I thought, well, it's seized. It took me some time to discover that the brakes had locked again. But I hadn't touched the brakes. The last time I touched them was going into the Casino square, just to steady the car. I talked to the Lockheed rep, and he said, "Well, I told them not to do this and I told them not to do that," and I said, "I thought you were in charge." He said no, so I went to see Raymond Mays and said, "I'm not doing you any good and you certainly aren't doing me any good, so we'd better part." It broke my heart – I had to pay them back a pretty hefty retainer, or the proportion of the races that I was due to do, which might have been six or eight. I had to duly deduct two races' worth and give them back the rest. It was a lot of money in those days. Three or four thousand pounds, plus they got very high starting money. The organisers were willing to pay BRM more than they'd pay me driving a 250F for a private entrant.'

The result was that when Moss informed Vanwall that his sinus trouble would keep him out of the two races in France, Vandervell and Yorke were able to contact Salvadori, who was at a loose end. When Brooks joined Moss on the casualty list, Stuart Lewis-Evans was engaged to bring the team back to full strength.

Driving the car for the first time over the Circuit des Essarts outside Rouen, Salvadori was not impressed. 'It didn't seem anything special. It was very quick, quicker than anything I'd driven before, and it didn't go at all badly, except we had this breather problem. The engine would breathe out the oil and it would squirt on to the circuit and on to your back tyres, which it did to me. It caused me a worry but it didn't cause me any damage. I know that

Flockhart in the BRM, who was following me, went straight off the road on my oil. Eventually I twigged what was going on. It was too difficult, so I came in and they retired the car. But it seemed OK. As a car I thought, "Well, that's not too bad." Not what I would choose. Nothing like the 250F Maserati that I'd driven previously, but it had lots of power.'

The seating position made him feel ill at ease. 'You were on top of the car, almost. You sat well down in the 250F. And you just had this feeling that you had to be extra careful. With the Cooper, you just threw it around. Sometimes it got away from you, but more often than not you felt in control of it. It was up to you what you did – you could use the throttle to move the back around. You didn't get that impression with the Vanwall, although it had more power. It was too restrictive, as far as I was concerned.'

He went on to Rheims not knowing how many more races he would be required for, but nevertheless in an optimistic mood. 'I knew the circuit very well, and I thought to myself, "This should be good." It was good, for Stuart, but for me the car was so tricky that it wasn't true. They'd put some very large wheels on my car, and I think that might have caused it. I said, "Well, I don't really want to drive this any more." But Stuart went extremely well. In those days we only had a few laps of practice because we were worried about the length of the race and we were worried about finishing, particularly with the Vanwalls, because I think up to that stage they'd hardly finished a long-distance race. So I had two different feelings: a good feeling from Rouen and a very indifferent feeling from Rheims. I think Stuart finished third and I finished fifth at Rheims, which wasn't too bad. Neither of us had finished at Rouen. But my impression was that they'd already got two of the best drivers they could have had for that car, in Moss and Brooks. It needed a lot of precision. It told you who was the master straight away. And from that point of view, Moss, who was the greatest driver in the world apart from Fangio, and Brooks – well, the car was almost tailor-made for those two.'

The Vanwall team had taken an extra car to France, with a special body designed by Costin, covering the wheels in the style of the 1954 Mercedes 'streamliner' but with a greater amount of genuine aerodynamic theory behind its shape. Manufactured by the Abbey Panel and Sheet Metal Company of Coventry to standards higher than Zagato managed when executing Costin's design for Moss's Maserati coupé, it was nevertheless no more successful. Salvadori and Lewis-Evans were still getting to grips with the basic car, and neither man felt comfortable enough to get the best out of the streamlined version during practice at Rheims, as Moss or Brooks might have done. Intended solely for use on ultra-fast circuits, it was put away and became an instant museum piece.

Lewis-Evans was kept on and the team expanded to three cars when Moss and Brooks returned in time for the British Grand Prix, but for the rest of the season Salvadori switched to the Cooper team. He had been driving for them, alongside Jack Brabham, in Formula Two races, and the team was gradually making the move to the top level. There was no question of negotiating over a contract. 'John Cooper would say, "Will you come and drive for me?" And you'd say, "Yes, John, I'd love to." And that was it. We used to collect our starting money at the foreign races. If you went back to England and waited for it to arrive, you might never see it or it might be months coming. But if you queued up on the

Monday morning after the race, you could collect it in readies and you'd know you'd got it and there was no problem. I did have a contract with BRM, but there was no contract with Vanwall, because it was too short-term. We used to believe each other. If you made a deal, you would stick by it. Otherwise the word would get around and I don't think anybody would particularly want to deal with you. There was a 50–50 split on prize money, less 10 per cent for the mechanics. That's what you'd live off. I don't think Jack and I got a retainer, or maybe a small amount, peanuts. But the main money would come from the petroleum companies. Both Jack and I were Esso runners, so we would get a large sum, certainly very large in those days compared to any other monies, and we'd get it on the first of January and that was our major lump, so to speak. Anything else was a supplement. Prize money was reasonably small. It's pathetic when you think of the sums that are spent on motor racing now. But nobody was complaining.'

Driving a two-litre Cooper in the British Grand Prix, Salvadori was delighted to find that he was more than a match for the Ferrari of Maurice Trintignant, an experienced Frenchman who had replaced De Portago. 'I kept passing him in this little car, I think I was in third or fourth position, and I'd get John Cooper coming out into the road and waving his fist at me saying virtually, "Go slower!" I'd think, "Oh no, I'd love to get in front of a red car again." So I'd pass again and I'd get another rocket from the pits. Maybe John was right, because the gearbox broke towards the end and I had to go very slowly and I finished in fifth position.'

That fifth place yielded two points, the first ever won in

the world championship by a driver in a rear-engined car, yet there was little in the way of celebration that night. 'It didn't really work that way. You got on with the next one. You'd be rushing back to the factory and Jack would be in charge of the preparation and I'd be trying to drum up another race and make suggestions. It was really from race to race.'

By comparison with the lavish facilities that produced the Vanwall, the Cooper operation was a modest one. 'We were working on a shoestring,' Salvadori said. 'We stayed at the cheapest hotels we could find. They never booked in advance, so you'd go round hunting for a hotel. Two or three of us would share a room. You'd always share a room with your team-mate. We'd share transport. John, Jack and myself travelled together, and the two mechanics arrived in a transporter. Jack would always give a hand, and so would I if I could do anything useful. We were workers as well. We'd have two cars and a spare gearbox, and maybe a spare engine, which would be sensible because you only got your starting money if you started, even if you only went a hundred yards.'

Sometimes they had trouble getting an entry for races on the Continent. 'Ferrari was the first car they wanted, then Vanwall, then Maserati, then BRM. We were right down the pecking order. They obviously thought we weren't much of an attraction, with our small engines. Even at the Nürburgring it was difficult to get an entry with the Cooper originally. You had to prove yourself. I remember one year they wouldn't let Jack in with a Formula One car. He had to drive a Formula Two car in the race. They said he hadn't got enough experience. Of course, he went like a bomb and led some of the Formula One cars. Once that happened, he was in.'

The Nürburgring was not really to Salvadori's taste. 'I did very well there, but to be truthful I was just a little nervous – or respectful, perhaps – because it was somewhere you could really come unstuck. There were trees everywhere, and if you went off the road and into the undergrowth they might be half a week finding you. I've known them be looking for a couple of hours for a car that had disappeared in practice. And there were very few marshals. It's so different today. So marvellous to be racing today.'

Aintree, Silverstone, Goodwood and Monza were among his favourite circuits. 'Rheims was very dangerous. Spa was a marvellous circuit, but you only made one mistake there. If you lost it, you were in big trouble. Our accidents used to go on for ever. These days, with their wide tyres, I've seen them spin cars here and within a few yards they've stalled them. The tyres just stop them. We'd go on for half a mile and collect everything that was in the way. Then you'd got the problem of fire. All these things you look back on now. In those days we didn't see them. Couldn't afford to. And therefore it didn't feel so dangerous. We were against safety belts because that was the thing that would get you killed. In front-engined cars, you have a shunt and the engine takes it, and moves right back through the gearbox and through the steering wheel. You were better off being thrown out. Your chances were greater. You never give a thought to being strapped in. I'm not sure we were right, but that was the thinking.'

At the Nürburgring, where each lap lasted ten minutes and a grid of a dozen cars would have represented poor value for the vast crowd camping and picnicking in the mountains, the field was expanded by allowing Formula Two cars to enter and running the grand prix for two classes. Cooper took two F2 cars for Brabham and Salvadori, but neither lasted the course. The Australian's transmission broke after seven of the 22 laps, while Salvadori lasted another five laps and was leading the smaller class when his suspension broke out on the circuit. That piece of bad luck enabled him to watch Fangio's epic pursuit of Collins and Hawthorn from a privileged vantage point.

'I don't remember where the car packed up, but I did maybe a mile hoofing it back to the pits and I saw it happening,' he said. 'I certainly wouldn't have seen what I saw from the pits. He was taking ten seconds a lap out of those Ferraris. Look, a second's a lifetime. When you talk about ten seconds, it's something you can't believe. It was incredible, he had the whole car moving, looking like it was out of control but actually in perfect control. You'd look at it and say, "He can't do that." But he did. He was driving like I'd never seen anybody drive before. He just picked up the time each lap until on the last lap he passed the two cars. Normally he was very placid. But he was really trying. And to say that about Fangio really means he was trying. It was incredible. And he was so loved. What did they do afterwards, those two drivers, Hawthorn and Collins? They were all over him. It was as if they'd bloody won. They were so thrilled, so thrilled, because everybody loved the guy. I reckon they got hell from Ferrari.'

After the race the Cooper team had to wait to get their starting money before leaving that night for England, where they were due at Brands Hatch the following morning for the August bank holiday meeting. 'It was the only way you could accumulate any money,' Salvadori remembered. 'We had to get from the Nürburgring to Dunkirk to catch the night ferry for practice, which started at seven o'clock in the morning. So after the race we try and get our starting money. No, we've got to go to the gala dinner, and we'll be paid after the speeches. This is not the place we want to be. Eventually we collect our scratch and about 9.30 or 10 o'clock we rushed to our cars. John Cooper was my passenger, trying to get to sleep, and I cannot tell you what a dice we had trying to catch that ferry and get a couple of hours' sleep before we got to Brands Hatch. It was pouring with rain in practice and we were at the back of the grid. I think I won the first section of the F2 race, had a big shunt in the sports car race and felt groggy, and that was the course of a day back then. That's the way it went on.'

A week later they were setting off for a resort town on the Adriatic, a destination unfamiliar to everyone in the team. While Brabham prepared for a lengthy stint behind the wheel of the transporter, Salvadori got into his borrowed Hillman Minx and set off to pick up Tony Brooks, his companion on the long drive south.

9

Practice

PERICOLO: the word needs no interpretation. All around the track it can be seen in red capital letters, the headline on more than a thousand posters warning spectators in precise terms of the dangers of motor racing. It is, after all, barely three months since innocent bystanders were slaughtered by the side of an Italian country road while watching the Mille Miglia, bringing down the wrath of the political and religious establishment on the world of motor racing.

Two days before the race, most of the drivers get up late. There is no official practice, so they plan to make a few exploratory laps in their road cars while the mechanics check over their racing machines. The Ferragosto fireworks kept many of them awake, those who were not lingering in the restaurants and hotel bars, until about half past one in the morning. ('A fantastic noise,' Denis Jenkinson notes in his diary, not meaning it kindly.) Stirling Moss, up at a leisurely nine o'clock, looks around the shops, goes for a swim, and spends the afternoon completing five laps in his rented Fiat.

Jean Behra is out in his Porsche, which bears the signs of an accident on the journey from Modena. Fangio is taking a look in a Lancia, as are Giorgio Scarlatti and Horace Gould. Brooks and Salvadori drive round in the Hillman Minx, which is getting a more thorough road test than usual. Gregor Grant goes along for the ride: every peasant in Pescara seems to be out with donkeys, mules and oxen, he notes. Denis Jenkinson picks up Michael Tee, *Motor Sport*'s young photographer, at the local aerodrome before reconnoitring the circuit in his Porsche.

Some of the English entrants express their surprise at the configuration of the circuit. The detailed map they received a few weeks earlier from the organisers, along with the race regulations, indicated that three speed-reducing chicanes would be used, as was the case when the Coppa Acerbo was run before the war. As a result, some of them did not bother to change their Nürburgring axle ratios. Now they are discovering that two of the chicanes have been removed, leaving only the third, which is placed at the very end of the sea-front straight, 500 metres before the pits. The decision to delete the chicanes was the subject of a communication from the organising committee, issued on 8 August, but not everyone seems to have received it. The changes mean that the cars will be running at peak revs in top gear for about ten kilometres on each lap, and a certain amount of recalculation is needed.

Brabham, brought up on Australian dirt tracks, has already developed an intense dislike of the place. In his view this narrow, poorly surfaced circuit is highly dangerous. He can't believe that racing can be encouraged through villages and between houses, along roads bordered by trees and telegraph poles. His car is bouncing up and down so hard on some of the rougher sections that it feels as though his helmet is about to fly off.

Brooks and his Italian fiancée, on the other hand, are enjoying the experience enormously. Most of the Vanwall team are quartered in a hotel on the seafront, just outside the town. Not counting friends and family, there are sixteen men and one woman in the official party at Pescara. Tony Vandervell has arrived in his company's De Havilland Dove with his pilot and his secretary, Marion Moore. There are the three drivers. There is David Yorke, the team manager; the chief mechanic, Cyril Atkins, and his number two, Norman Burkinshaw; and six other mechanics, plus two engine specialists. The cars have arrived in a pair of well-equipped transporters, the newer of them introduced at Rouen two months earlier.

When Bruce Halford and his mechanic, Tony Robinson, arrived in Pescara, they tried to park their rather humbler transporter – a converted Leyland Royal Blue coach – on the beach, thinking that they, too, could spend the weekend sleeping by the sea, but without paying hotel prices. They were settling down when visitors in uniform arrived. They had chosen the site used for the municipal firework display, and were invited to move elsewhere. Now Halford is driving the coach round and round the circuit, trying to memorise its features.

Bernard Cahier is enjoying the company of the Maserati squad, sharing a hotel with Fangio, Behra, Schell and the rest. Nothing unusual in that. This is an era in which a driver will bump into a journalist and say, 'What are you doing for dinner?' Joan Cahier, who normally takes her husband's longhand manuscripts and types them up for *Road & Track* in the US, *Motor Racing* in England, *Auto Revue* in Switzerland, *L'Automobile* and *Action Automobile* in France, *Auto Moto und Sport* in Germany, and *Autovisie* in Holland, is at home, looking after their two small children. For once, she will not be available to comfort any wife or girlfriend of a driver involved in an accident.

After their reconnaissance laps, most of the drivers swim and shop before preparing for dinner in one of several excellent seafront restaurants. Luigi Musso, however, is hanging about with an anxious look on his face. Then, late in the evening, a red transporter pulls up and three mechanics get out, ready to unload a Ferrari 801. At last he can be sure he is in the race.

Two practice sessions are scheduled for Saturday. The first takes place between seven o'clock and half past nine in the morning, and the second from half past four until half past six in the afternoon. Between the sessions the straw bales are removed and the circuit is opened to traffic in order to allow the population and the holiday-makers to go about their lawful business. Nevertheless Michael Tee, taking photographs from a corner at the end of one of the short straights up in the mountains, notes the sight of a goatherd taking his flock across the road while one of the sessions is in progress.

Meanwhile the teams are discovering another unexpected and unusual problem, caused by the decision to locate the start line exactly halfway along the pits. On a circuit measuring 15 miles, there is no question of either a warm-up or a slowing-down lap. For those teams with a pit beyond the start line, it will be necessary to get the mechanics to push the car back quite a long way so as to give the driver time to get it up to a decent speed as he crosses the line to start the lap, in order to be given a time. Otherwise one whole lap will be wasted. And at the end of a run all the drivers, wherever their pits are located, have to come to a screeching halt as soon as possible after the finish line and then wait for their mechanics to come and push them back. 'Wonderful to behold, with cars going in all directions,' Denis Jenkinson notes.

Straight away Moss gets down to the business of finding out which of the four Vanwalls suits him best. The number one driver has the right to try his team-mates' cars and, if necessary, to swap with them for the race. To take advantage of the long straights, Moss's own car has been fitted with a high rear axle ratio and the largest tyres available, giving a potential maximum of 173mph at 7200rpm. But the car will pull no more than 6900rpm, probably the equivalent of around 160mph, and the road-holding is vague. The car feels as though it is wandering. To the relief of all three drivers, however, the severe problems experienced at the Nürburgring have been cured.

Half an hour before the end of the morning session Moss jumps into Lewis-Evans's car. Even though it is geared to reach only 162mph at a maximum of 7200rpm, he finds it a great improvement. Back at his hotel by mid-morning, he has a bath and lunch while the mechanics go to work. At half past four, when some of the heat has gone from the day, he returns to the pits and sets off again, this time in Brooks's car, which is prone to overheating but will reach 7300rpm. His own engine is showing the signs of piston trouble, and his best time, 9min 54sec, is set in his number two's car.

This, however, is all of 10 seconds slower than the time with which Fangio has claimed pole position. The world champion is driving a lightweight 250F with the chassis number 2529, the car he drove in Buenos Aires and Rouen and at the Nürburgring. No one is surprised to see him at the front of the grid, but 10 seconds seems an awful lot, even over a 15-mile circuit. Among the Vanwall team there is a strong feeling, perhaps encouraged by Moss's inside knowledge, that Maserati have given Fangio a specially powerful brew of fuel to use in practice, probably including nitromethane. The English drivers can only hope that such a potent recipe will be unsuitable for use in a long-distance race.

A hugely relieved Musso, the winner of the last Formula One race at Pescara three years ago, is third fastest in 10min 00sec, having done more laps than anyone. Behra is fourth in 10.03, Schell fifth in 10.04, Brooks sixth in 10.08. Lewis-Evans is a disappointing eighth in 10.29 – curiously, since the third Vanwall seems to be the fastest car of all on the straight (Gregory, an impressive seventh on the grid, is claiming that when Lewis-Evans passed him, the Vanwall was going at least 20mph faster than the Centro Sud Maserati). A persistent problem with the fuel injection pump on Lewis-Evans's car was finally sorted out when the team owner himself adjusted it to the correct setting, using a half-crown coin and guesswork. Scarlatti, due to drive a new Maserati with a V12 engine, has abandoned it in favour of a car fitted with a conventional six-cylinder unit and has qualified no higher than ninth. Fangio and Behra have both tried the experimental car, but neither is convinced of its power advantage. Piotti, at the wheel of the only private 250F tuned to run on methanol, is 13th. Salvadori and Brabham, their little Formula Two cars running out of breath on the long straights, bring up the rear of the grid in 15th and 16th places, more than a minute and a half slower than Fangio. The large gaps indicate the unusual nature of the circuit and its unfamiliarity to many of the drivers. Both Brooks and Lewis-Evans, deprived of their cars for a proportion of the practice sessions, leave the circuit that evening with the belief that they could have gone faster.

Moss takes an early evening meal and a bath, climbs into bed at 9.15pm and sleeps well. Others are not so fortunate. 'Supper,' Jenkinson writes in his diary, 'then bloody fireworks.'

10

The Race

On Moss's watch, mounted on a distinctive strap made of two thin steel bands and worn on his right wrist, the hands are moving towards half past nine. In front of the pits, which are constructed from scaffolding poles, with a balcony for spectators above the working area, the crews gather a few feet from the cars as the drivers wait, revving their engines. Over on the other side of the track, the grandstand is packed; fights are occasionally breaking out when the occupancy of seats is disputed, requiring the forceful intervention of the uniformed *carabinieri*.

In the VIP tribune are the members of the honorary race committee, led by no fewer than three joint presidents: Avvocato Giuseppe Sparato, a parliamentary deputy; Professore Giovanni Iannucci, leader of the town council; and Dottore Antonio Mancini, of the local chamber of commerce. Around them sit officers of the Automobile Club di Pescara and other members of the committee, including two senators, two more deputies, the chief of police, and the presidents of the committees of agriculture, industry and tourism.

Some spectators are reading that morning's edition of

L'Abruzzo e Molise, the local paper, which celebrates the running of the 25th Gran Premio di Pescara with a series of special features. It lists the field, profiles the drivers (including, vainly, the absent Collins and Hawthorn), gives the full results of all the previous 24 races, and provides a lap chart for spectators to fill in. The main story is devoted to Fangio, described in the headline as 'L'Abruzzese di Buenos Aires': his grandparents emigrated from the Abruzzi mountains to Argentina in the last years of the 19th century, which means that the five-times world champion is, to all intents and purposes, a local boy. A panel on the front page announces that another special edition, containing a full report of the race, will be available two hours after the contest ends. For the benefit of those holiday-makers who will be staying on, a list of forthcoming local attractions includes the Coppa Gino Celidonio for professional cyclists on 1 September, the election of Miss Italia and Miss Cinema 1957 in the Arena Florida on 3 September, and an exhibition of contemporary art at Francavilla al Mare, featuring works by Morandi and Modigliani.

A comfortable-looking man in a white shirt, dark slacks and beach shoes, wearing a white cyclist's cap against the sun, appears at the side of the track next to Fangio's car. This is Dr Mario Rutolo, the race director. He is carrying a flag. His appearance is the only warning that the start is imminent. Newspapers are hastily laid aside. Marshals and photographers stand expectantly on the straw bales placed on the edge of the road to protect the front of the grandstand. A Maserati mechanic who has been exchanging last-minute words with Fangio moves hastily back over the white line that demarcates the pit lane. Now the engines of the cars on the first few rows are roaring. The temperature is rising. Dr Rutolo raises the flag, and lowers it with a flourish.

Musso, pride and ambition blazing, shoots away first, on the outside of the front row, leaving black streaks of rubber on the road. He is followed by Fangio and Moss, while Behra makes a rapid getaway from the second row and Gregory pushes the white-and-blue Maserati between Schell and Brooks. Fangio and Moss are side by side behind the lone Ferrari as they cover the crowded kilometre before the first bend, with Behra in close attendance.

Behind the leaders, the grid is in chaos. As the flag falls, mechanics are still attending to some of the cars at the back of the field. Most of them manage to dodge between the Maseratis and Coopers as the drivers get away, but one unfortunate is caught by Gould's car and is flipped into the air, landing on the bonnet of the 250F. Gould slams on his brakes and watches as the mechanic slides off the bonnet, gets to his feet and retreats to the pits. Then he lets out the clutch, floors the throttle pedal and roars off in pursuit of the pack, into a haze of dust and smoke.

To help identify the drivers in teams with more than one car, the noses of certain cars are painted in different colours. Moss's Vanwall has a white band round the nose, while Brooks's and Lewis-Evans's are left plain green. In the Maserati team the noses are yellow for Fangio, blue for Behra and white for Schell. Curiously, the sole Ferrari appeared with a plain white nose-band in practice but now has a thin red stripe added for the race: perhaps a way of indicating to the authorities that this is a private entry and that its appearance does not indicate Enzo Ferrari's willingness to climb down from his high horse.

As the leaders swing through the big 90-degree right turn

that will take them up the hill and out of the town, the world champion takes precedence. But the fast-starting Behra, with his tail up, overtakes the Vanwall and his own team leader and goes through into second place. By Villa Montani, the Frenchman has thrust the blue nose of his Maserati ahead of the Ferrari. Behind them come Fangio and Moss. As they weave through a series of sinuous uphill bends, Musso finds a way past Behra, and he is leading as they roar through Spoltore, with its narrow streets and its sharp right turn slap in front of the village church.

After Spoltore the cars plunge downhill to a small plateau. Now Moss is challenging Fangio and Behra. As they climb again through Fornace towards Cappelle, he takes the world champion, whose car is carrying a heavy load of petrol, around twenty gallons. Through the streets of Cappelle Moss is on Behra's tail, and as they approach the spectacular hairpin bend at the exit from the village he dives inside the Maserati, holding the high-tailed green car a few millimetres away from the black-and-white-striped kerbing as he slides around the turn, giving the hundreds of spectators on the grass bank above the corner something to remember.

Moss is directly behind Musso as they roar downhill along the first of the long straights, past the hamlet of Mulino towards the seafront at Montesilvano. Using the Ferrari's horsepower, the Italian driver stays in front as they brake for the right-angled turn on to the flat coast road, joining the main highway from Ancona to Bari. For almost two minutes they hold the throttles to the floor, the cars touching 170mph as they blast between the houses, the shops and the crowds towards the chicane. Behind them are Fangio, Behra, Brooks, Lewis-Evans, Gregory,

Bonnier, Schell, Scarlatti, Godia, Salvadori, Brabham and Halford. Lewis-Evans has overtaken Gregory on the straight, confirming the American's impression of the Vanwall's speed. There is no sign of Piotti, who has abandoned his car in the hills around Cappelle, its engine blown. Gould, desperately trying to make up for ground lost in the mayhem of the start, arrives at the chicane travelling far too fast, slams into the straw bales and ends up under a tree, his race over.

When the cars emerge into the sight of the grandstands, a huge cheer goes up. Ten minutes after he disappeared down the road, Musso is still in the lead. He roars past the pits with Moss three seconds behind, followed at a distance of a further 13.8sec by Fangio. Behind them, a green car pulls into the pits. Brooks's Vanwall is overheating: a broken piston is eventually diagnosed, and the first of the English cars is out. The driver is sorely disappointed: this is the sort of track he could have got his teeth into.

But Musso's great patriotic effort cannot last. As they begin the second lap, Moss closes up. Now the Vanwall is on the Ferrari's tail. Denis Jenkinson, who has chosen to watch the race from the mountains, notes the way Moss is putting the difficult Vanwall into smooth power slides, although from his vantage point on a high bank he can look down into the cockpit and see how hard Moss is working at the steering wheel to make those slides seem effortless. As they roar down towards the sea, however, Moss draws abreast of Musso and then pulls ahead. The Italian is dismayed: he glances down at his rev counter and sees that the needle is flickering past the red line, which is marked at 9000rpm. He is travelling at close to 170mph, but Moss is going a good 5mph faster. When they come past the grandstand for a second time, with the green car in the lead by just under two seconds, the reaction is more muted. In the Vanwall pit, the stopwatch shows that Moss has just lapped in 9min 46.4sec, 8 seconds faster than his best practice lap and representing an average speed of just over 98mph.

By this time Michael Tee, travelling across country on the back of a motorcycle, has reached his vantage point just outside Capelle. He clambers up a bank and waits for the cars to come round so that he can start taking his photographs. Although he is some way from the village, there are plenty of spectators picnicking at the roadside.

Fangio is already 26 seconds behind the flying Vanwall. Is this unusually sizeable gap just a result of his usual dislike of leading the early stages of a race, or is the world champion taking it easy, knowing that his title is in the bag? Is he suffering from the use of a less potent nitromethane mixture than the one that produced his shatteringly quick lap in practice? Or is he banking on Musso yet again driving his machinery to destruction in the quest for glory, and on the Vanwalls falling victim to the mechanical frailty that has so frequently curtailed promising performances? His own 250F is a sturdy car, built for exactly these conditions. He has plenty of fuel; he is in a good position; he can bide his time and wait to see how things turn out.

All the way around the third lap, Musso attempts a furious counter-attack. Dust and stones fly up from the loose verges as the two cars slide together around the mountain corners. At the end of the third lap, the Vanwall is still holding a narrow lead. Half a minute later, as Lewis-Evans passes the pits in fifth place, a tread flies off the nearside rear tyre of the third Vanwall. This is an occupational hazard at high speeds in high temperatures, when tyres overheat and small cuts or manufacturing flaws are exposed, but the unfortunate timing means that the driver has to nurse his car around the whole circuit at rapidly diminishing speed on three good tyres and one wheel with the remains of its Pirelli Stelvio flailing around the rim. By the time he returns to the pits and the mechanics rush to hammer off the winged hubcap and fit a replacement wheel, he is at the back of the field.

Another green car has failed to complete the third lap at all. Brabham and Salvadori have been having a gentle dice at the back of the field, neither of them particularly enjoying the experience. The 1.5-litre engines in their little Coopers can give them no more than 145mph on the long straights, about 30mph slower than the front-runners, even though the extra fuel for this long-distance race, carried in expanded aluminium tanks, gives them a bit of extra momentum on the downhill section. Another benefit from those aluminium tanks is already disappearing fast. On a hot day the long-range tanks, placed along the rear-engined car's flanks, by the side of the driver's legs, and under the scuttle above his thighs, help to keep him cool in the early stages of the race. While reeking horribly, sometimes from tiny leaks, the fuel retains its low temperature. At Pescara, as the sun rises higher in the sky, the drivers are grateful for that. But when the tanks start to empty, the aluminium heats up very rapidly. By the end of the race, if they get that far, the drivers are sitting in a furnace, the sides of the tanks scorching their legs through their overalls as their cars slide through the bends and they are pushed sideways by G-forces in the cramped cockpit. Meanwhile there is probably a small leak somewhere, and the reek of fuel grows even stronger. 'All that is going on,' Salvadori says, 'and you're thinking . . . well, you don't want to think about it, actually. You're much better forgetting about it.'

Having discovered that they cannot match the performance of the bigger cars, Salvadori and Brabham contemplate the sensible idea of pacing out a nice quiet race and cantering home to collect whatever small prize money is available to the more lowly finishers. But they are racing drivers, after all. In close company, and left to their own devices, they start behaving like racing drivers, which is to say they race each other, going quicker and quicker in their internecine battle, partly for fun and perhaps in frustration at their inability to challenge anyone else.

Around the back of the circuit, on the twisty stretches between the villages, some of the earth verges are coming loose as the cars clip the apexes and slide wide on the exits. Salvadori is running just ahead of his team-mate, which is the best place to be in a battle with Brabham, who already enjoys a reputation for employing the dirt-track habits of his youth, sliding wide and showering anyone behind him with debris. Black Jack, they call him, and that is one of his specialities.

On the third lap Brabham pushes the nose of his Cooper alongside Salvadori, and then falls back. Salvadori glances in his mirrors to check his team-mate's whereabouts. Momentarily, his concentration is broken. Suddenly the back end of the car is sliding. Now he, too, is running wide, so wide that his outside rear wheel slams into one of the sturdy stone kilometre posts that line the roads from which this circuit was made. Salvadori gets going again, but the wheel is wobbling and he can only tour round to the pits.

Brabham gets there first and pulls in to shout the news to John Cooper. When Salvadori eventually arrives, he gets out of the car and has a drink. The mechanics examine the car and discover that the impact has bent a suspension arm. Salvadori is out. Somewhat relieved, he finds a large piece of cardboard which he will wave at his team-mate the next time the surviving Cooper comes past. On it he scrawls two words: GONE SWIMMING.

After three laps, Moss is 3.3sec ahead of Musso. A lap later the gap is 7 seconds, with Fangio a further 34 seconds in arrears. Now Behra, the star of the first couple of miles, drops back from fourth place and cruises into the Maserati pit. The bonnet is taken off the 250F and Guerino Bertocchi peers inside. Behra takes off his crash helmet. The mechanics make adjustments and restart the engine, but the clattering noise makes it clear that the Frenchman, too, is out. Now Gregory is fourth, hotly pursued by Schell, who is making up for his poor start.

Moss's lead continues to expand. As they pass the pits for the fifth time, it is 8.8sec. Schell overtakes Gregory. Scarlatti is sixth, a minute behind the American. Bonnier's bodywork appears to have come loose and his car is over-heating; after two pit stops fail to produce a cure, he calls it a day. On lap six Moss is 10.6sec ahead, but Lewis-Evans comes into the pits again, this time with his offside rear tyre in shreds.

With seven laps gone the Vanwall is 13.8sec in front of the Ferrari and 1min 1.4sec ahead of Fangio's Maserati. Then come Schell, Gregory, Scarlatti, Godia, Halford, Lewis-Evans and Brabham, who has just been relegated to last place again. The next time round, Moss's lead is 16 seconds and Musso's oil filler cap can be seen to be flapping open. Frantically his crew signal for him to come into the pits at the end of the following lap. But after Moss has passed the pits again, Musso simply continues the apparently vain chase, having lost another three seconds to the Vanwall and apparently oblivious to the instructions. Moss is pressing harder and harder, and covers his ninth lap in 9min 44.6sec, matching Fangio's pole position time.

The consequences of Musso's failure to heed the signals from his pit become apparent on the tenth lap. His oil tank has split and he begins to leave a trail around the circuit. By the time he reaches Cappelle and the start of the descent to Montesilvano, the oil has run out. Deprived of lubricant, the V8 engine seizes solid and Musso's defiant effort is at an end. Neither he nor the Ferrari has been good enough to challenge the combination of Moss and the Vanwall on a classic road circuit, but his spirited performance wins the sympathetic applause of the spectators as he emerges from the cockpit, removing his travel-stained goggles, helmet and gloves. It falls to Mino Amorotti, the team manager, to find a telephone and break the bad news to Enzo Ferrari, back in Maranello.

Moss, however, cannot ease off yet. In Germany two weeks ago Fangio produced the drive of his life to overhaul Collins and Hawthorn, who thought they had the old man beaten. Maybe he has been playing cat and mouse again. And, indeed, he has just started to speed up when fate takes a hand. At Cappelle, he fails to spot a patch of Musso's oil and he loses control. As his car spins round, the nearside rear wheel clouts the stone wall. Brabham, who has just been lapped, watches it happen. At the end of the lap Fangio comes into the Maserati pit at a much reduced speed, the car's shapely tail displaying a large dent and the wheel wobbling badly. Fortunately, nothing structural is damaged. The mechanics fit a new wheel and Nello Ugolini sends the world champion on his way, now nearly three minutes behind the Vanwall and no longer in a position to strike back.

Nor can Gregory mount a counter-attack on Schell's third place, since his scuttle is coming loose. He keeps going at barely reduced speed, but two more Maseratis disappear from the scene when Halford's transmission fails at the end of the tenth lap and Godia's engine gives up a few minutes later.

With seven of the eighteen laps still to go, and more than an hour and a quarter of racing left, Moss is under no threat. He can concentrate on getting the car home, knowing that petty mechanical failures – a fractured high-pressure pipe here, a broken throttle cable there – have cost the Vanwall dear in earlier races. For the crowd, the spectacle is almost over. Unlike the screaming V8 Ferrari and the rasping straight-six Maserati, the four-cylinder Vanwall does not announce its arrival with a signature wail. Its long, elegant single exhaust pipe, emerging from four blended outlets on the left side of the tapered bonnet, creates little more noise than that of a large, well-bred family saloon. The contrast seems symbolic: the disciplined competence of Vandervell Products is about to record a significant triumph over the more highly strung temperaments and intuitive methods of the Scuderia Ferrari and the Officine Alfieri Maserati.

In the hills, where breezes have kept the temperature down to around the 90-degree mark, there are long gaps now between the cars. Michael Tee watches the crowd get up and walk around. The sound of an approaching Maserati gives them time to clamber back to safety. A purring Vanwall, however, is on them almost before they know it, leading to flurries of activity and mothers scurrying back to collect small children who have been left behind in the path of the oncoming car. There is nothing to drink but wine. Tee has been warned against the local water. He tries the wine, but it only serves to make him thirstier.

There is a scare for the Vanwall team when, without warning, Moss pulls into the pit at the end of the 13th lap. The oil pressure gauge has been fluctuating, and the mechanics whip off the bonnet to pour extra lubricant into the tank. Moss takes a swift drink of water – the time is approaching noon, and the fierce sun is at its zenith – before easing the heavy gear-change into first and setting off again after a stop of 54 seconds.

Even though the leader's lap times have dropped to around 9min 53sec, and despite encouragement from his pit, Fangio still seems unable to match Moss's pace. There is nothing he can do now except wait for the Vanwall to hit trouble. And in that respect the Maserati team can take encouragement from a new problem confronting Lewis-Evans, whose throttle is sticking. Several times he arrives at corners still on full throttle, frantically trying to brake against the engine's effort. Eventually he devises a method of switching the ignition on and off, which at least allows the brakes to act only against the weight of the car, rather than taking on 270 brake horsepower as well. Lapped by Moss and having a generally miserable day in the unbear-able heat, he thinks of giving up. But ahead of him Scarlatti is in trouble, pulling into the pits with an engine problem and a burnt-out clutch. The Vanwall pit urge him to carry on in an effort to snatch fifth place from the Maserati.

Moss takes it even easier over the last two laps, maintaining a gap to Fangio of around three minutes. When he crosses the line for the 18th and final time, after 2hr 59min 22sec of racing, only Fangio, Schell and Gregory are still on the same lap. Lewis-Evans makes it into fifth place, some consolation after a morning filled with tiresome interruptions, ahead of Scarlatti in sixth.

Seventh and last is Brabham, who has circulated virtually on his own since the disappearance of Salvadori. The Australian, too, has been having a pretty dismal morning: he is the only finisher to have been lapped twice, despite making no pit stops. He ends his race, however, on a lighter note. As he turns into the coastal straight to complete his final lap, his engine starts to splutter. Despite its long-range tanks, the Cooper is running out of fuel. Before long the splutter has turned into a cough, and eventually the engine dies altogether. Coasting along the Via Adriatica, Brabham spots a petrol station, closed for the morning while the race is on. 'I can park it there,' he thinks to himself, 'and walk to the pits.' But as he coasts silently into the forecourt, a man in overalls and a large smile emerges from behind the pumps. Jumping to attention, he makes it clear that he recognises the problem and is keen to help. Brabham jumps out, shows him where the filler cap is, waits for the man to put in three or four litres, shakes his hand and pulls away to finish the race.

As Moss crosses the line, acknowledging Dr Rutolo's chequered flag, he slows and pulls into the Vanwall pit. Sadly, there will be no lap of honour. The circuit is too long. Instead the celebrations begin.

Hot and weary, his face and his bare forearms covered with a fine deposit of oil and dust, Moss pulls down his goggles, climbs out of the car and removes his gloves. Someone hands him a bottle of San Pellegrino. He and Vandervell embrace: twice now they have beaten 'those bloody red cars' – first with the aid of a bit of luck on home ground at Aintree and now, fairly and squarely, on Italian soil. Moss has set a new race average of 96.08mph to beat the record of 88.66mph set in 1933 by Luigi Fagioli in an Alfa Romeo, and has established a new lap record, eclipsing the mark set in 1932 by none other than Tazio Nuvolari's Alfa and now left at 98.44mph. These records were set on a circuit devoid of chicanes, which is why they lasted through the pre-war era of German supremacy. Now, as he did in the Mille Miglia two years ago, Moss has rewritten the records on Italian roads.

He has also lifted himself into second place in the championship table, above the grieving Musso. Moss is taking the congratulations of his father, of Brooks (who has been sitting on the pit counter with Pina since his retirement) and of his crew when Fangio drives across the line and brakes to a halt. The world champion climbs from the cockpit, waits for the mechanics to come and start pushing the car back to the Maserati pit, and then walks along to the Vanwall pit, where he gives Moss a warm embrace. No one has a better understanding of what this victory signifies.

Home

By lunchtime, the day was over. The race organisers could congratulate each other on a well-run event without casualties among competitors or spectators. The chaotic scenes on the starting grid were already forgotten. The mechanics cleaned up the cars, collected the wrecks, loaded them all into their transporters and started to think about the journey home to Acton, Surbiton, Modena or Maranello. Around the circuit, the straw bales were removed from junctions and the roads began to return to normal. Bicycles, tractors, Fiat Topolinos and donkeys carrying sheaves of hay once again moved over the roads where Moss, Musso, Fangio and the rest had spent three hours in high-speed combat.

The journalists went around chatting to the drivers and team managers, collecting their impressions. In an era before television monitors covered the whole circuit, it was the only way to find out what had happened. For Bernard Cahier, his first visit to Pescara had been a wonderfully memorable experience. 'The atmosphere was great in those days,' he said. 'The smells, everything. The cars sounded different. Nowadays they all sound the same. And there was something about those cars, the Vanwalls and especially the beautiful Maserati 250F, in the surroundings of a place like Pescara. The photographs looked like paintings. I watched the race from different places. Some shots in the town, at the start, and then I'd walk maybe a kilometre. You could walk anywhere. You could cross the track, if you wanted. We never thought about an accident. My camera was a Leica 3G, which I bought in 1953, with a 135mm lens – the biggest you could fit on that camera. There were maybe 20 or 30 journalists, and not even that many photographers. I remember the people in Pescara were enthusiastic and very helpful. They were fanatics. And you didn't have to worry about anything being stolen.'

That night the drivers and teams attended the post-race function, after which the private entrants could collect their starting money. 'There was the usual banquet,' Pina Brooks said, 'which I remember as being very jolly and noisy, full of life and enthusiasm, like all Italian motor racing activities. People were trying to chat me up not just because I was a woman, but because I was Brooks's fiancée. Stirling was very happy because he had won, I remember that.'

Journalists were also invited. 'Nobody left after the races in those days,' Cahier said. 'We all stayed for a reception and sometimes for a dinner. It was wonderful for journalists because we had a good chance to meet and talk to the drivers and to get stories. In those days there wasn't a rush.'

Tony Brooks contrasted it with the behaviour of later generations of drivers. 'Of course we stayed around afterwards,' he said. 'There was none of that getting into your helicopter in a huff and flying off to your Monaco pad. It was courteous to attend the dinners. And they were fun.

Drivers spoke to each other, instead of disappearing into their million-pound mobile homes. No wonder they hate each others' guts nowadays. They never communicate. And if you don't communicate, you can imagine all sorts of terrible things about the opposition. If there was any non-sense in the race, we'd sort it out at the dinner. Communication solves most of the problems of this world.'

Moss left for Rome at 11 o'clock that night, accompanied by his father in the rented Fiat 1100. Less than halfway there the car blew a gasket; the frugal Moss recorded in his diary that a taxi for the remaining 120 miles cost 10,000 lire. Their BEA plane was cancelled, so they took an Italian airline flight an hour later. 'Took off at 4.10am. No bed. Arrived in London 8.15.' Moss went straight to his flat in Challoner Mansions, had a snack, unpacked his case and went off to his office. After lunch he returned home, repacked his bag, waited for Katie and her friend Margo to arrive, and at 5.45pm took a car to London airport, where he took off at 7.15pm on a Pan-American Airlines flight to New York, stopping briefly at Shannon in southern Ireland, where he visited the duty-free shop. 'I bought a Rolleiflex for $112, which was obviously a very good deal.' Four days later he was streaking across the white wastes of Utah's Bonneville salt flats, breaking speed records in a tiny teardrop-shaped MG.

While Lewis-Evans set off back to England in his absurd little Nash Metropolitan, Salvadori prepared for the return journey with Tony and Pina Brooks. But this time there would be an extra body. Brabham left the transporter to the mechanics and hitched a lift in the Hillman Minx.

'It was quite an exciting trip,' he remembered in a

deadpan tone. 'I'd just finished paying the bill at the hotel and when I came out everybody was in the car. There was only one seat vacant, and that was behind the steering wheel. I assumed that meant I had to drive. I'd only been driving for a few miles and we were passing a big truck and there was a chap on a motor scooter and he was also passing it. As I went past him, Roy leaned over and grabbed the steering wheel. The chap on the scooter thought he was going to be pushed under the truck. He wasn't very pleased. A little while later we were stopped at a level crossing and he caught us up. It was a right-hand-drive car: Pina was in the front and Roy and Tony were in the back. As the chap drew up, he spat in what he thought was the driver's window, all over Pina. He got off the bike and started writing down the registration number of the car. The barrier went up and we set off, but after a little while there was another level crossing and we had to stop again. He caught up and started to have another go. Well, the blockage cleared and we were on our way again. Then we came up behind a convoy of military trucks who were holding everything up. I had a go at passing a couple of them, but we came up behind a policeman on a motorbike who was riding alongside in the other lane to stop anyone going through. Tony told me I wasn't being aggressive enough. He said he'd take over. I stopped the car. "Pass me my gloves," he said. He got behind the wheel and set off.'

Brooks's version begins with the military convoy. 'It stretched ahead as far as the eye could see. It had a motor-cycle police escort, and when there was nothing coming towards us they'd move to the centre of the road to stop people even trying to overtake. We followed this for 10 minutes or a quarter of an hour, far too long. Jack was driving, and I said to him, "Jack, they're going all the way up the Adriatic road – they could be going all day. We'll never get to Milan tonight. It's not good enough." He refused to do anything about it. I said, "Jack, get out of the seat." Roy was in the front passenger seat and he must have held the steering wheel while Jack got out of the seat and I got in. I was just so fed up with it. So we relegated Jack to the back seat and just after some oncoming traffic had made the police motorcyclist move in behind the convoy, I accelerated past him before he could move back out again. Then I went harry flatters, passing all these trucks – I don't know how many there were, but they stretched into the distance – 20, 30, maybe 50. The motor-cycle policeman didn't reckon this at all so he set off after us. I think Jack was a bit worried in the back and I don't think Roy was as confident as he usually is, but I just drove hell for leather, giving this car a proper road test. I just kept going and this guy was going harry flatters behind us and what happened was that, very fortunately, it started to rain. I didn't slacken my pace at all but the police motorcyclist didn't reckon it too much, so I gained a bit of an advantage. Eventually we got to the front of the convoy and we still kept going. He kept on after us and what he would have done to us if he'd caught us, I don't know. Fortunately there was this level crossing ahead of us. The lights were going. The barrier was going to come down. I said, "Well, if we stop here, we're all in jail." I don't know how close the old barrier came to the car but we just went underneath it and it closed in time to cut off the policeman. Thank goodness, that was the last we saw of him. I kept going, though. He might have been one of those persistent guys. And my adrenalin was pumping so hard I couldn't have dropped down to a normal pace anyway. It sounds like *Boys' Own* stuff, but it's absolutely true – my wife remembers it vividly, and I'm surprised she married me after that, frankly.'

About an hour later, in Brooks's account, they came to a road with a loose gravel top. 'I was still pumped up and I don't think I'd slowed down a lot, and we overtook a scooter, and maybe the odd stone hit his scooter or hit him or something. Again we came to level crossing. The barrier was down this time, so we pulled up. And apparently to make this scooter man even more angry, Roy had given him a V-sign. I'd gone past him quite normally – I had no intention of spraying him with stones. I think it was the V-sign that got him really wound up, not the stones. He caught up with us at the level crossing and assumed that it was the driver who'd given him the V-sign. I had the window down and he came alongside and spat at me. I got my arm up just in time to get the spit on my arm rather than on my face. Salvadori, of course, was killing himself in the passenger seat, because it was he who'd caused the international incident. We did get to Milan that night and left Pina with her family. Roy stayed somewhere. I don't know what happened to Jack. I think he must have gone off somewhere. Perhaps he didn't reckon my driving, or being relegated to the back seat.'

That night Denis Jenkinson sat up until 2.30am writing his report, which ran to 3500 words. His labour did not go uninterrupted. 'Bloody fireworks twice,' his diary noted. The next morning he gave his manuscript, five or six sheets of foolscap paper covered in small, neat longhand, to Michael Tee and drove his colleague to the aerodrome, where the photographer climbed into the vacant seat in the mail plane. At midday Jenkinson left Pescara in convoy with Jesse Alexander, both of them in their little Porsche coupés, heading for Modena through rainstorms and heavy traffic.

With a former fighter pilot of the Italian air force at the controls, Tee took off for Rome. As they approached the imposing massif of the Abruzzi, with the plane already close to its ceiling, Tee noticed with some concern that they were heading for the side of the mountain, some 300ft below its ridge. They were almost on it when suddenly the pilot muttered something to himself and pushed the joystick sideways, throwing the plane on to its side. As they banked away from the mountainside, he explained to his shaken passenger that usually a natural updraft carried him over the ridge. On this day, however, the extraordinarily hot weather had messed up the airflow and they were in for a long detour around the mountain.

Gianni Marin, the correspondent of *Auto Italiana*, had also stayed up working on his report. 'From the last-minute arrival of the authorisation for the race to the near-boycott by Enzo Ferrari as a result of his recent problems following the Mille Miglia,' he wrote, 'many problems – most of them bureaucratic – had to be overcome by the enthusiastic organisers of the 25th Gran Premio di Pescara. In the end their passion, their goodwill, their abilities and their desire achieved a triumph, offering motor sport a practically perfect setting in which to hold a race that took place in the best and safest possible conditions.' He also praised the winning English car and driver, allowing not the slightest hint of chauvinism to betray his disappointment in the performance of the Italian teams. 'We have been given a demonstration of Moss's great qualities,' he wrote. 'His calmness, confidence and perfect style showed him to be in top form, physically as well as technically. This was an amply merited victory.'

At home there was joy and satisfaction in an historic success. 'If Aintree was the turning point in British grand prix fortunes,' an *Autosport* editorial announced the following Thursday, 'Pescara set the seal on the progress of Vanwall by Stirling Moss's near runaway win on the difficult Adriatic circuit. The prestige of British automobile engineering is ever on the upgrade, and by defeating the Italians no less than twice in world championship events, Mr G. A. Vandervell has done a tremendous service for the entire motor industry in this country. Just as the Schneider Trophy performances many years ago brought fame to British aviation, the Vanwall achievements in the most advanced form of automobile technology have created a profound impression on all who are concerned with the distribution of motor vehicles. The term "Buy British" has certainly become one of real significance . . .'

Autocar was no less excited. 'In winning his second *grande épreuve* for Tony Vandervell in less than a month,' the magazine's correspondent wrote, 'Stirling Moss has placed Britain once and for all among the leaders in grand prix racing. It has taken four years of patient effort . . . and now the rewards are coming in.'

American enthusiasts read the words of Bernard Cahier in *Road & Track*: 'Vanwall's splendid victory in Pescara was fully deserved and certainly more convincing than their other big victory at the British GP last July. The Pescara circuit is not only a "driver's course", but also a terrific test of reliability as well as speed. The two Vanwalls of Moss and Lewis-Evans were the fastest in the straight and they withstood without difficulty the terrible punishment of this circuit . . .'

To Roy Salvadori, however, the victory was less of a surprise. 'Why shouldn't Moss have won? He was the equal, virtually, of Fangio. In sports cars, I reckon, in those days the master would have been Moss. So why hadn't he won before? That was the surprise.'

Back in Acton, the celebrations were not allowed to disrupt the normal working of the team. After a cheque from the Automobile Club di Pescara was received at Martin's Bank in the City of London, the accounts for the payment of the drivers were prepared under the supervision of Marion Moore, Vandervell's secretary (and, later, his third wife).

Moss's cheque for £1850.17s.6d broke down as follows: £625 retainer, £500 starting money, £494.5s.5d in prize money, £82.7s.5d for fastest lap, £20 from the BP bonus, £36 from Ferodo, £30 from KLG and £9 from Hepworth and Grandage, 'less 30,000 lire (£17.3s.3d) advanced in Pescara to S. Moss and 50,000 lire (£28.12s.1d) advanced in Pescara to A. Moss.' Brooks's cheque, for his proportion of the starting money, came to £429.1s.3d. Lewis-Evans received £382.14s.3d, made up of £357.11s.0d in starting money and £82.6s.5d in prize money, less the deduction of an advance of £22.17s.9d and a Pescara hotel bill of £35.5s.5d for three nights.

All Vanwall's suppliers took out advertisements in the motoring magazines, emphasising their part in the success: 'The winning Vanwall was fitted with Ferodo disc brake friction pads and clutch linings. On his own cars, Stirling Moss always uses Ferodo.' At the beginning of the season, BP had made the first of two payments of £3000 to the team, 'on the understanding that you will be using our BP fuel and Energol lubricating oils in all competitions'. Now their investment was showing a dividend.

12

Then

Three weeks later they met up again at the Monza auto-drome for the last *grande épreuve* of the season. Moss triumphed again, this time over the full Ferrari team – Musso, Hawthorn and Collins – as well as the Maserati squad. That made three victories in the year, and two of them on the Italians' territory. The Vanwalls had empha-sised the point by starting the race from the first three places on the grid. A month later, his fame having reached a new peak, Moss married Katie Molson at St Peter's Church, Eaton Square, amid a scrum of newspaper photographers. After a reception at the Dorchester Hotel, they left for a honeymoon in Amsterdam.

Pescara and Monza had been the last races of an era. Wanting a closer identification with their customers, the petrol companies had pressed for a change in the rules on fuel. Their products could be promoted more effect-ively, they believed, if grand prix cars raced on something close to the stuff available at ordinary filling stations, which for the big teams meant a complete rethink on how the engines were tuned and an acceptance that a loss of power would be incurred. In future, if you wanted the acrid fumes and explosive combustion of nitro-methane, you would have to go to a drag strip. For 1958, too, the race distance would be reduced from 500 to 300 kilometres, or from three hours to two. No longer was a grand prix to be a test of endurance as well as speed: at the top level, motor racing was taking the first steps towards tailoring its proportions to the attention span of a television audience.

Nevertheless 1958 was to be a season of even greater success for the Vanwall team, who took the very first FIA constructors' championship, with the same three drivers at the wheel. Moss won for the team at Zandvoort, Oporto and Casablanca (and in Buenos Aires, driving a Cooper), while Brooks claimed wins at Spa, the Nürburgring and Monza: 'the three classics', as he would proudly say four decades later. Fangio finally retired midway through the season, yet Moss still missed the drivers' championship by a single point. It was Hawthorn who claimed the distinction of becoming the first British world champion, after a season in which two of his team-mates died in races: Musso at Rheims and Collins at the Nürburgring.

And in the last race of the season, Stuart Lewis-Evans was killed when his Vanwall's engine seized on a fast stretch of the Mellaha track in Casablanca. The car hit a tree, bursting its petrol tank and starting a blaze from which the driver was pulled with severe burns. Moroccan medical care was not up to the task, and Vandervell's private plane took Lewis-Evans back to England, where he was treated by the specialist burns unit at East Grinstead Hospital. On 25 October, six days after the race, he died.

A year earlier, perturbed by Lewis-Evans's lack of stamina, Vandervell had sent him to Harley Street for an examination. A duodenal ulcer was identified. 'We used to carry bottles of milk with us everywhere,' said Bernie Ecclestone, who travelled with him for much of the season. 'But it never bothered him. He never had an operation and he kept it under control. He was bloody quick, just a nice kid who wanted to race. A bit different from the way they are today. Vandervell certainly thought a lot of him. You couldn't not think a lot of him. I think his accident was the beginning of the end for Vanwall. You know, when somebody's killed and they hit the wall and die instantly, that's bad enough. But this was different. I remember being with him in his hospital in Casablanca – he was sitting in a chair with a blanket round him, waiting and waiting for a doctor. Bernard Cahier's brother, who was a doctor, saved him from that. But he was in the hospital for a while before he was flown home.'

For Vandervell, the tough, demanding industrialist, the personal tragedy meant nothing less than the end of his commitment to motor racing. He had driven out to the Mellaha circuit proudly at the head of a line of three Van-walls, each driven by a mechanic in spotless white overalls, a team as impressive in its presentation and performance as the Mercedes outfits of earlier eras. But at the moment of his greatest triumph, the death of Lewis-Evans destroyed his passion. Moss and Brooks were told they would be free to find new teams for 1959. Over the following three seasons cars bearing the Vanwall name made a total of only four appearances, and the tepid nature of the effort was out of keeping with the whole-hearted intensity of the earlier operation. A Vanwall raced for the last time at Silverstone in June 1961. Vandervell himself died in 1967, and the company he had created was sold. Moss's Pescara car, which carried chassis number VW5, had long since been broken up.

Grand prix cars were not to be heard again in the mountain villages or along the coastal roads around Pescara. The 1957 race, arranged at short notice, was never repeated. In fact there was no race at all until 1960, when the 26th Gran Premio di Pescara was held for the new Formula Junior cars, featuring such stars of the future as the New Zealander Denny Hulme and the young Italian trio of Lorenzo Bandini, Lodovico Scarfiotti and Giancarlo Baghetti. A year later a final event, a four-hour race for sports cars in the style of the old Targa Abruzzo, was won by a Ferrari with Scarlatti and Bandini, a veteran and a novice, sharing the wheel. Enzo Ferrari had won the first race held there, and a car bearing his name won the last.

The following year, on Easter Monday 1962, Stirling Moss suffered serious injuries at Goodwood, driving a Lotus. It was the end of a racing career that contained many unforgettable displays of skill, courage and competitive spirit. Although Pescara may not have been his most demanding or dramatic victory, none of the others had more significance, or a more mythic quality. And there was never a race quite like it again.

The title of this book is intended to convey an emotional truth rather than a literal one. The more rigorous motoring historians will point out that road racing did not actually end on 18 August 1957. Over the next few years, world championship grands prix continued to be held at places such as Rheims, Rouen, Oporto, Avus and Monsanto; and, of course, the circuit around the houses at Monte Carlo remains in use to this day, as does a shortened version of the great Spa-Francorchamps track. At Le Mans, sports cars still use sections of public roads for the 24 Hour race. Pau, too, continues to host an annual single-seater race on the circuit that winds through its streets. Over the last 20 years the cars known as Indy Cars or Champ Cars, originally built for oval circuits, have made increasingly regular appearances on the streets of US cities. In the 1980s there was even a Formula Two race around Birmingham's Bull Ring.

Nevertheless the race at Pescara marked the end of a certain philosophy of road racing. No longer would massed-start races, on open roads from town to village and back again, be organised in that *ad hoc* way, without permanent facilities or even the vaguest notion of safety precautions. In mainland Italy, the reverberations of the Mille Miglia tragedy more or less put an end to road racing. Even in Sicily, amid a semi-autonomous culture, the Targa Florio, the last of the great time trials, gradually withered away. For everyone involved, Pescara was an adventure – and, as it turned out, an unrepeatable one.

Pescara was real, in every sense. So real that it is still there, almost 50 years later, available for exploration by those who find themselves in that part of Italy and who would like to drive the roads where Moss, Fangio, Musso and the rest once did battle in their beautiful machines. Up into the hills, through Spoltore to Cappele and back down to the sea, there is little to impede a precise evocation of all the races that were ever held there.

Musso was killed at Rheims in 1958. Lewis-Evans died of the burns suffered at Casablanca that same year. Behra hurtled off the Avus banking to his death in 1959. Schell was killed in practice at Silverstone a year later. Gould died of a heart attack in 1968, aged 47. Bonnier's life ended in a collision at Le Mans in 1972. Gregory succumbed to lung cancer in 1985, aged 53. Fangio, Scarlatti, Piotti, Godia and Halford lived on into old age. They were no angels, most of them, but they lived by a set of values that included honour, patriotism and an acceptance of mortal risk. Even the most famous among them were not overwhelmed by their celebrity. They kept a sense of proportion that allowed them to maintain normal relationships with the rest of humanity. The 15 miles of road that start and end in Pescara, and the images of the great race of 1957, are their memorial.

Published Sources

Anonymous: 'British Victory – Italian Sunshine' (*Autocar*, 23 August 1957)

——: 'Grande Epreuve No 7' (*Motor Racing*, October 1957)

Cahier, Bernard: 'Gran Premio di Pescara' (*Road & Track*, November 1957)

Carri, Luca Delli: *Gli Indisciplinati* (Fucina, 2001)

Casucci, Piero and Tommaso Tommasi: *25 Anni di Formula 1* (Arnoldo Mondadori, 1975)

Chula, Prince: *Dick Seaman – A Racing Champion* (G. T. Foulis, 1941)

Colombo, Gioachino: *Origins of the Ferrari Legend* (Haynes, 1987)

Court, William: *Power and Glory: A History of Grand Prix Motor Racing 1906–1951* (Macdonald, 1966)

Curami, Andrea and Piero Vergnano: *La 'Sport' i suoi artigiani* (Giorgio Nada, 2001)

Edwards, Robert: *Stirling Moss – The Official Biography* (Cassell, 2001)

Fangio, Juan Manuel, with Marcello Giambertone: *My Twenty Years of Racing* (Temple Press, 1961)

Ferrari, Enzo: *My Terrible Joys* (Hamish Hamilton, 1965)

Francis, Alf, with Peter Lewis: *Racing Mechanic* (G. T. Foulis, 1957)

Grant, Gregor: 'Vittoria della Vanwall' (*Autosport*, 23 August 1957)

Henry, Alan: *Ferrari – The Formula One Cars* (Hazleton, 1984)

Jenkinson, Denis: *The Maserati 250F* (Macmillan, 1975)

———: *Jenks – A Passion for Motor Sport* (MRP, 1997)

———: 'XXV Gran Premio Pescara' (*Motor Sport*, September 1957)

Jenkinson, Denis, and Cyril Posthumous: *Vanwall* (Patrick Stephens, 1975)

Lyndon, Barré: *Grand Prix* (John Miles, 1935)

McKinney, David: *Maserati 250F* (Crowood Press, 2003)

Marin, Gianni: 'Rinconfirma Della Vanwall' (*Auto Italiana*, September 1957)

Merlin, Olivier: *Fangio* (Batsford, 1961)

Monkhouse, George: *Motor Racing with Mercedes-Benz* (G. T. Foulis, 1949)

———: *Grand Prix Racing* (G. T. Foulis, 1953)

———: *Mercedes-Benz Grand Prix Racing 1934–1955* (White Mouse Editions, 1984)

Moss, Stirling: *Stirling Moss's Second Book of Motor Sport* (Cassell, 1958)

Moss, Stirling, with Doug Nye: *My Cars, My Career* (Patrick Stephens, 1987)

Nixon, Chris: *Racing the Silver Arrows* (Osprey, 1986)

Nye, Doug (ed.): *Dick and George – The Seaman–Monkhouse Letters 1936–1939* (Palawan Press, 2002)

Owen, David: *Targa Florio* (Haynes, 1979)

Pritchard, Anthony: *Maserati – A History* (David and Charles, 1976)

Schmidt, Giulio: *The Roaring Races* (Edizioni della Libreria dell'Automobile, 1988)

Small, Steve: *Grand Prix Who's Who, 3rd edition* (Travel Publishing, 2000)

Thompson, Jonathan: *The Ferrari Formula One Cars 1948–1976* (Aztex, 1976)

Acknowledgements

My thanks go to Sir Stirling Moss, Tony Brooks, Roy Salvadori and Sir Jack Brabham for their time and memories. To Doug Nye, nonpareil racing historian, for his encouragement and for allowing me to see Tony Vandervell's correspondence and Denis Jenkinson's diaries. To Nigel Roebuck, whose enthusiasm persuaded me that I was not alone in my interest in this remarkable race. To Jabby Crombac, who put in a good word. To the wonderful Bernard Cahier. To Pino Allievi of *La Gazzetta dello Sport*. To Stephen Tee and Peter Higham, who allowed me to examine the LAT archive at Haymarket Press. To Michael Tee. To Rob Wiedenhoff of *Autovisie*, who made his own pilgrimage. To David Luxton and Richard Milner, who commissioned the book. And to those who were there in Pescara in the third week of August 1957, and who left us their impressions: the grand prix correspondents of *Motor Sport*, *Autosport*, *Motor Racing*, *Autocar* and *Auto Italiana*.

Entry

2 Juan Manuel Fangio (Argentina) / Maserati 250F / Officine Alfieri Maserati
4 Jean Behra (France) / Maserati 250F / Officine Alfieri Maserati
6 Harry Schell (France/USA) / Maserati 250F / Officine Alfieri Maserati
8 Giorgio Scarlatti (Italy) / Maserati 250F / Officine Alfieri Maserati
10 Francesco Godia (Spain) / Maserati 250F / Francesco Godia Sales
12 Luigi Piotti (Italy) / Maserati 250F / Luigi Piotti
14 Masten Gregory (USA) / Maserati 250F / Scuderia Centro Sud
16 Joakim Bonnier (Sweden) / Maserati 250F / Scuderia Centro Sud
18 Horace Gould (Britain) / Maserati 250F / H. H. Gould
20 Bruce Halford (Britain) / Maserati 250F / Bruce Halford
22 Roy Salvadori (Britain) / Cooper-Climax T43 / Cooper Car Co.
24 Jack Brabham (Australia) / Cooper-Climax T43 / Cooper Car Co.
26 Stirling Moss (Britain) / Vanwall / Vandervell Products Ltd
28 Tony Brooks (Britain) / Vanwall / Vandervell Products Ltd
30 Stuart Lewis-Evans (Britain) / Vanwall / Vandervell Products Ltd
34 Luigi Musso (Italy) / Ferrari 801 / Scuderia Ferrari

The Starting Grid

Front row

Musso	Moss	Fangio
(Ferrari 801)	(Vanwall)	(Maserati 250F)
10min 00sec	9min 54.7sec	9min 44.6sec
		156.49kph/97.81mph

2nd row

Schell	Behra
(Maserati 250F)	(Maserati 250F)
10min 04.6sec	10min 03.1sec

3rd row

Lewis-Evans	Gregory	Brooks
(Vanwall)	(Maserati 250F)	(Vanwall)
10min 29.6sec	10min 26.1sec	10min 08.6sec

4th row

Scarlatti	Bonnier
(Maserati 250F)	(Maserati 250F)
10min 36.6sec	10min 36.2sec

5th row

Piotti	Godia	Gould
(Maserati 250F)	(Maserati 250F)	(Maserati 250F)
11min 10.6sec	11min 09.8sec	10min 49.6sec

6th row

Salvadori	Halford
(Cooper-Climax T43)	(Maserati 250F)
11min 24.2sec	11min 16.3sec

7th row (centre)

Brabham
(Cooper-Climax T43)
11min 35.2sec

The Results

18 laps of 25.578km/15.99 mile circuit: 460.42km/287.76 miles.

1 Moss (Vanwall/VW5) 2hr 59min 22.7sec, 153.77kph/ 95.46mph
2 Fangio (Maserati 250F/2529) 3hr 2min 36.6sec
3 Schell (Maserati 250F/2527) 3hr 6min 9.5sec
4 Gregory (Maserati 250F/2502) 3hr 7min 39.2sec
5 Lewis-Evans (Vanwall/VW7) 3hr 7min 27.8sec, 17 laps
6 Scarlatti (Maserati 250F/2501) 3hr 9min 37.1sec, 17 laps
7 Brabham (Cooper-Climax T43/FII-5-57) 3hr 6min 40.5sec, 16 laps

Fastest lap: Moss 9min 44.6sec, 157.51 kph/98.44mph.

Retirements: Piotti (Maserati 250F/2519) lap 1, broken valve; Gould (Maserati 250F/2514) lap 1, accident; Brooks (Vanwall/VW6) lap 1, broken piston; Salvadori (Cooper-Climax T43/FII-8-57) lap 4, accident; Behra (Maserati 250F/2528) lap 5, broken valve; Bonnier (Maserati 250F/2507) lap 8, transmission failure; Musso (Ferrari 801/D50A-0003) lap 10, oil leak/engine failure; Godia (Maserati 250F/2524) lap 11, broken differential; Halford (Maserati 250F/2509) lap 11, crankshaft failure.

Index

Campari, Giuseppe, 15, 16, 58
Cannes, 27
Cappelle sul Tavo, 14, 20, 110–12, 116, 135
Caracciola, Rudi, 7, 18, 20
Casablanca, 132, 135
Castagneto, Renzo, 46
Castelfusano, 35
Castellotti, Eugenio, 68, 69, 80; killed, 70, 72; Moss on, 72–3
Catania, 46
CAV, 76–7
Chapman, Colin, 28, 30, 31, 43, 79
Chevrolet, 41
Chiribiri, 13
Chiron, Louis, 18, 64
Chula, Prince, 19
Circuit des Ardennes, 38, 40
Circuit des Essarts, 92
Circuito de Bologna, 39
Circuito del Polesine, 13
Circuito del Savio, 13
Collins, Peter, 25, 32, 80, 131; Monaco accident, 30, 52, 70; attitude, 34, 63; caught by Fangio at Nürburgring, 56, 70, 98, 116; joins Ferrari, 69; 1957 championship points, 71; Moss on, 72–3; excluded from Pescara, 74, 108; drives early Vanwall, 79; drives Cooper, 85; killed, 132
Connaught, 29, 45–6, 48; bankruptcy, 73
Cooper, Charles, 84, 86
Cooper, Elsie, 84
Cooper, John, 43, 78, 84–5, 86, 94–6, 99, 115
Cooper Car Company, 84
Cooper team, 5, 57, 94, 97, 98; difficulty entering races, 96
Coopers, 1, 9, 84–6, 93, 95, 132; at Pescara, 109, 113–15, 119; Cooper-Alta, 28; Cooper-Bristol, 85
Coppa Acerbo, 7, 13, 15, 17, 21, 58, 101

Coppa Florio, 38
Coppa Gino Celidonio, 108
Cortese, Franco, 17
Costin, Frank, 30, 79, 94
Côte d'Azur, 30
Coventry, 94
Coventry Climax, 86
Croce de Piave, 13
Croydon, 31
Cuba, 29
Cunningham-Reid, Noel, 53

D'Annunzio, Gabriele, 12
d'Argentina, Beria, 13
Daily Express International Trophy Race, 80, 91
Daimler, 37, 76
De Filippis, Maria Teresa, 72
De Havilland, 79; Dove, 54, 102
De Portago, Alfonso, 69, 95; crash, 70–1
Deauville, 31
Dei, Guglielmo, 64, 65
Delage, 16
Delehaye, 21
Dieppe, 39, 40
Docker, Lord and Lady, 31
Don, Kaye, 84
Doña Eva Duarte Perón Grand Prix, 59
Donington Park, 40
Dovercourt, 89
Dreyfus, René, 21, 63
Dunkirk, 99

Ecclestone, Bernie, 5, 48; television deals, 51–2; on Lewis-Evans, 83, 133
Ecurie Bleue, 63
Edge, S. F., 39, 84
Energol lubricating oils, 130
engine position, 43, 95, 97
ERA, 16; G-type, 28
Esso, 95

Fagioli, Luigi, 16, 18, 22, 29

Ugolini, Nello, 61, 117
United States, 29; development of motor racing, 37–8; racing colours, 64

Valspar, 51
Vanderbilt Cup, 38
Vandervell, Tony, 28–9, 32, 50–2, 73, 84, 92, 132; background, 75–6; bearings, 75, 77; relationship with Ferrari, 76, 78; Moss on, 76; early racing car developments, 77–82; at Pescara, 102, 120, 128; ceases motor racing, 133; death, 133
Vandervell Products Ltd, 77–8, 117
Vanwall team, 5, 33, 50, 55, 61, 63, 70, 92, 95; beginnings, 79, 82–3; atmosphere, 83–4; expands, 94; at Pescara, 102, 105, 118; suppliers' support, 129–30; 1958 success, 132
Vanwalls, 1, 9, 32–3, 44, 53, 64, 70, 72, 73, 84, 87, 91, 96, 122, 131; acceleration, 28, 82; bodywork, 30; breather trouble, 92–3; cease racing, 133; colours, 109; design, 28–30, 52, 93–4; at Pescara, 109–12, 115–18, 128; racing car developed, 79–82; reliability, 29,

81, 93, 112, 117; seating position, 93; special body, 94; speed, 104, 111, 128; suspension, 33, 56, 75, 82
Varzi, Achille, 16, 18; death, 72
Vatican, 71
Viareggio, 89
Villa Montani, 110
Villa Raspa, 14
Villa St Maria, 14
Villoresi, Luigi, 23, 46, 59, 67; at Pescara, 64; retirement, 72
Volpate, Signor, 26
von Brauchitsch, Manfred, 7, 20

Walker, Rob, 86
Wallis, Barnes, 42
Wharton, Ken, 79
Willesden Green, 76
world championship, 3, 4, 7, 8, 22, 28–9, 81, 89, 132; first points for rear-engined car, 95–6
Wyer, John, 82

Yorke, David, 32, 55, 81, 92, 102; Moss on, 82

Zagato, 30, 94
Zandvoort, 132

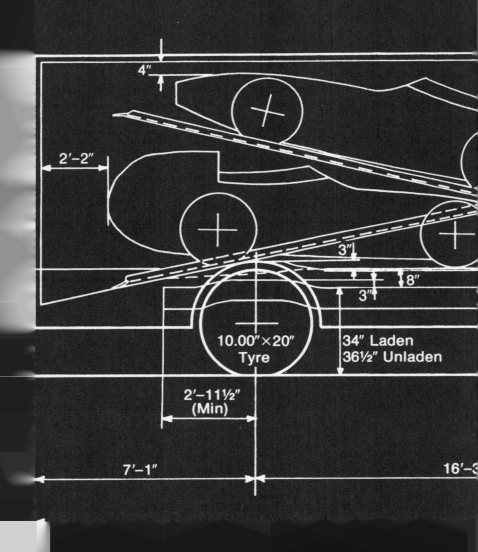

4″

2′–2″

3″

8″

3″

10.00″×20″
Tyre

34″ Laden
36½″ Unladen

2′–11½″
(Min)

7′–1″

16′–3